The Victorians: A Very Short Introduction

VERY SHORT INTRODUCTIONS are for anyone wanting a stimulating and accessible way into a new subject. They are written by experts, and have been translated into more than 45 different languages.

The series began in 1995, and now covers a wide variety of topics in every discipline. The VSI library currently contains over 700 volumes—a Very Short Introduction to everything from Psychology and Philosophy of Science to American History and Relativity—and continues to grow in every subject area.

Very Short Introductions available now:

Available soon:

For more information visit our website

www.oup.com/vsi/

Martin Hewitt

THE VICTORIANS

A Very Short Introduction

OXFORD
UNIVERSITY PRESS

OXFORD
UNIVERSITY PRESS

Great Clarendon Street, Oxford, OX2 6DP,
United Kingdom

Oxford University Press is a department of the University of Oxford.
It furthers the University's objective of excellence in research, scholarship,
and education by publishing worldwide. Oxford is a registered trade mark of
Oxford University Press in the UK and in certain other countries

Published in the United States of America by Oxford University Press
198 Madison Avenue, New York, NY 10016, United States of America

British Library Cataloguing in Publication Data
Data available

Library of Congress Control Number: 2023930845

ISBN 978–0–19–873681–3

Printed and bound by
CPI Group (UK) Ltd, Croydon, CR0 4YY

Contents

Acknowledgements

This study emerges out of several decades of thinking about the Victorians, encouraged at the outset by Asa Briggs's idiosyncratic but always stimulating doctoral supervision, and then confirmed by the investment in Victorian Studies made with the loyal backing of Christine Hallas and other colleagues at what was then Trinity and All Saints College, Leeds. The demands of an inaugural lecture for the professorship of Victorian Studies to which the college appointed me did much to coalesce the ideas about the Victorian as period summarized in Chapter 2, and students on undergraduate and MA courses helped me refine the ideas there and in Chapter 1.

Over the years I've also drawn insight and inspiration from colleagues and collaborators involved in the *Journal of Victorian Culture*, the British Association for Victorian Studies, and at Manchester Metropolitan, Huddersfield, and Anglia Ruskin universities, far too many to mention. I'm especially grateful to Patrick Leary, Tom Crook, and Susie Steinbach for reading drafts, and to Joanne Shattock, Isobel Armstrong, Peter Mandler, Helen Rogers, Rohan McWilliam, David Amigoni, and the late and much-missed Simon Dentith, Malcolm Chase, and Rosemary Mitchell for assistance and encouragement with other work on which this volume has drawn.

For all this, without the repeated patience of the VSI commissioning editors at OUP, and then the support of the Principal and Fellows of St Hugh's College Oxford, who elected me as the first Belcher Visiting Fellow in Victorian Studies in 2019, and then adjusted and extended the fellowship in response to the disruptions of COVID-19, it is doubtful whether the book would have been completed. I hope this portrait is a fitting return for the hospitality of the St Hugh's community and the generosity of Margaret Belcher in funding the Fellowship.

The Victorians

List of illustrations

Chapter 1
The challenge of generalization

A century ago, when the Victorian age had scarcely begun to be a focus of scholarly examination, perhaps the most influential of all studies of the period opened with the provocative assertion that 'The history of the Victorian Age will never be written. We know too much about it.' A hundred years later even though they have largely passed out of direct memory, it remains even more the case that we know too much about the Victorians to render them in 35,000 words without systematic and often flagrant simplification.

Every characterization in the pages which follow is defenceless against the challenge that it underestimates complexity, smooths over unevenness, and excludes difference, that it offers a 'totalizing account' which would dissolve on closer scrutiny. Indeed any impression to the contrary must be tenaciously resisted. The reader should be under no illusion. Victorian Britain was a mass of tensions and contradictions, of inconsistencies and incompatibilities, of instabilities and competing subjectivities. It was fiercely insular *and* determinedly global; the railway age and the heyday of the horse; both smug and anxious; a time of extraordinary change but also of remarkable continuities, producing enormous wealth and pitiless poverty. Patterns were always under construction; conventions never uncontested. All characterizations of the Victorian—and in particular all formulations of what 'the Victorians' did or thought—in the pages that follow must be read as prefaced with a silent 'on balance', 'on the whole', or 'predominantly', omitted in the interests of economy and elegance.

None of this inevitable historical messiness is any reason not to generalize or to attempt to sketch the broad patterns and norms around which diversity was arrayed, and this is especially so in the case of the Victorians. Partly because Victorian culture was shared across all classes and groups to a remarkable extent, the intellectual life of the period profoundly structured by pervasive underlying assumptions, languages, and reference points. Partly because Victorian Britain was marked by particularly powerful social norms and expectations, bearing down on, to a greater or lesser extent, all parts of society. Partly because in exploring the shades and balances of the period, writings about the Victorians, including those by the Victorians themselves, have very often begun with a general interpretation which they have proceeded to dismantle or subvert. The Victorians, as the historian John Darwin has put it, 'agreed on generalities but differed in detail', and it is only by comprehending the general pattern that we can fully understand the nature of the diversity.

As historians have long recognized, one of the most difficult challenges in studying any period in the past is getting a sense of the particular combination of ways of thinking and ways of living which characterized it. This is perhaps especially true of 'the Victorians' because the Victorian period has been the site of a set of particularly rich engagements from a variety of perspectives, which have not always, indeed perhaps rarely, successfully balanced the two poles of *thinking* and *living*.

In what follows I have tried to develop a portrait of the period which explores the mutually constitutive operations of experience, action, and reflection. I do so by addressing five questions which seem to me to be critical in approaching the Victorians. Why do we continue to be fascinated by the Victorians? How does the Victorian age work as a historical period? What was distinctive about it, what gave it its particular character? Who were the Victorians, as individuals and collectivities? How far were those phenomena we might describe as 'Victorian' a global presence in the 19th century?

Beyond this, the aim here has been to be as capacious as space will allow, and to extend the cast of individual Victorians presented in the discussion as far as possible. This requires a certain allusiveness and even abruptness. Some of the individuals appearing in the following pages will be familiar, others less so, but in either case there has been little time for introductions. While their significance for the argument should be apparent, the fullness of their example may have to be the subject of further investigation.

Chapter 2
Living with the Victorians

What is it about the Victorians? Over 120 years after the death of Queen Victoria they still command a degree of attention and occupy a place in British and indeed global culture which no other period in history can match, possessing a cultural significance and carrying a degree of ideological freight without parallel. It isn't hard to recognize from the ways that the term 'Victorian' is used in contemporary debates and discourse that it is rarely a neutral designation like '19th century'. Rather it is almost always a loaded term. While most period designations, even 'Elizabethan' or 'Georgian', are denotative and might describe a body of literary work or a style of furniture, 'Victorian' is connotative, laden with associations and meanings. Not surprising, then, that the Victorians not only have their own '-ism' but also have their homologue, 'Dickensian'.

Why are the Victorians unique in this respect and what are the consequences?

There are several obvious reasons. The length of the reign, the longest in British history before it was surpassed in the 21st century by Elizabeth II, has something to do with it, as do elements of nostalgia for a time when Britain was the dominant global superpower, and western versions of culture and progress were spreading rapidly across the globe. But equally important is the seemingly perpetual presence of the Victorians, the extent to which despite enormous effort they have never been safely consigned to the past, so that we continue to feel ourselves cohabiting with them. In Britain in particular, the history of the 20th century looks at times like one long and largely unsuccessful struggle to escape, of the fear expressed by the mid-century poet and writer David Paul that 'We have not succeeded...in relegating [the Victorians] to a glass case. They refuse to stay in the case.'

'It remains true', Paul added, 'that in most Englishmen today [he was writing in 1952] you can still find an ill-concealed Victorian.' The same might have been said about colonial societies and other parts of the anglophone world. And of course, although the Victorian period might have ended in 1901, the Victorians themselves lived on. Even restricting the designation to those who were 21 in 1901, it was not until 1955 that Britain had its first post-Victorian prime minister. Winston Churchill's leadership in the Second World War, William Beveridge's conception of the British welfare state, Frederick Lugard's classic development of 'indirect' imperial rule in Africa were all in this sense Victorian. The architect of mid-century macro-economic orthodoxy, John Maynard Keynes, was himself only six months shy of 18 when Victoria died, and older more firmly Victorian thinkers lived on to shape western intellectual life, even when they professed to repudiate the Victorians. The philosopher Bertrand Russell, born 1872, continued to publish until the year before his death in 1970.

Even as the youngest Victorians passed away indirect influences remained. In his autobiography, the British Conservative prime minister John Major recalled the formative presence of his own Victorian father, born in 1879, who had 'a tireless fund of evocative stories that stretched back well into the nineteenth century'. The historian Asa Briggs, whose writings and talks established the orthodox view of the Victorians for much of the second half of the 20th century, and who was brought up in inter-war Keighley, which he remembered as 'very much a Victorian community', conceded that he was himself 'a bit of a Victorian'. And intimacy with the great Victorians was constantly replenished through the final third of the century by a new breed of monumental biographies, typified by Robert Blake's *Disraeli* (1966) and Gordon Haight's *George Eliot* (1968), in which psychology replaced piety or prejudice, and the Victorians became flesh and blood.

As the Victorians died off, their material legacies lived on. Commentators who set out to capture the essence of 20th-century Britain were struck by the extent to which it bore the impress of its Victorian past. J. B. Priestley's *English Journey* (1934) offers a classic presentation of a Britain saturated with Victorian survivals, from eccentric manor houses straight out of Dickens, to industrial regions clinging to the vestiges of Victorian prosperity. Painted around the same time, *Victorian Survival* (1931) by the American painter Grant Wood offered a parallel reflection, juxtaposing a forbidding great-aunt with the telephone as contrasting forms of endurance. In Britain in the 1960s slum clearances, and even the 'Beeching axe' which led to the closure of over 2,300 railway stations and 5,000 miles of railway lines, only tinkered with these survivals. The national railway network, the sewage and sanitation system, the housing stock and urban morphologies, all remained predominantly Victorian. At the end of the century British popular bestsellers and television shows were still exploring 'What the Victorians Did for Us', or 'the Victorian-ness of the world in which we live'. And this is without the vestigial Victorianism of the eponymous Victorian brands the British consumer continues to buy—Rimmel cosmetics, Cadbury's chocolates, and Colman's mustards—or the Tennyson Avenues and Crimea Streets in which some continue to live. If outside Britain such material legacies were less obvious, there were still innumerable everyday survivals, postage stamps and photographs, policemen and detectives, department stores and museums, golf and tennis, bacon and eggs and breakfast cereals, bicycles and telephones, Christmas cards and valentines.

Intellectual legacies also appear almost anywhere one looks. Our everyday language is full of Victorian coinages: 'dinosaur', 'scientist', 'colour prejudice', even the concept of 'normal'. The British version of parliamentary democracy and the Houses of Parliament as its embodiment are both essentially Victorian. British welfare policies and institutions continue to be powerfully influenced by the sorts of assumptions which were enshrined in the Victorian Poor Law. The British film classification regime and the variants implemented by almost all its settler colonies are to all intents an extension of Victorian approaches to the censorship of books and plays.

It was once conventional to argue that despite the forces of inertia the sexual and generational revolts of the 1960s brought 'The End of Victorianism'. But the 1960s counter-culture had a surprisingly complicated relationship with the Victorians, repudiating their puritanism and prudery, but gravitating to 'Victorian' neighbourhoods in cities like San Francisco, absorbing Victorian dress into hippie style, drawing inspiration from all sorts of Victoriana, from the Pre-Raphaelite influences of Led Zeppelin's lead guitarist Jimmy Page to the scraps of Victoriana running through the Beatles' 1967 *Sgt. Pepper's Lonely Hearts Club Band* album. Imperial pretensions were abandoned, but only by force, and beliefs about the incapacities and inadequacies of colonial peoples and minority populations remained virtually unquestioned not just up to but well beyond independence, as the challenges of the 2010s, the Windrush scandal and the Black Lives Matter movements, show.

Certainly the 1960s did nothing to dent the pre-eminence of the Victorians in the anglophone cultural canon. In many respects the opposite. After 1918 the reputation of the Victorians had gone into steep decline. Cleaner modern lines swept away old decorative styles, and Victorian art and literature, condemned for their sentimentality, was not far behind; paintings by first-rank artists were sold off for just a few pounds. But this almost 40-year eclipse proved temporary, and by the 1950s, the tide was turning again. Victorian architecture was once more appreciated, the market for Victorian art rebounded, communities repackaged and relaunched their Victorian museums and heritage attractions, and Victorian literature consolidated its position as the default playbook for costume drama in film and television. The 'Main Street U.S.A.' attraction at the early post-war Disney theme parks was a nostalgic celebration of American small town life at the very end of the Victorian period. A host of late 20th- and early 21st-century novelists, including Margaret Attwood, Peter Ackroyd, Peter Carey, Beryl Bainbridge, and Amitav Ghosh, have excavated the Victorian condition in fiction. The extraordinary frenzy of attention prompted by the centenary of Victoria's death in 2001, from the major Victorian Britain exhibition at the Victoria and Albert Museum in London, to satellite events like the Tate's Victorian Nudes, did nothing to exhaust appetites, as the willingness of museum curators across the English-speaking world to give space to an ever-extending variety of Victoriana, from Victorian photocollage (Chicago, 2010) to 'badass rebel women' of the era (New York Museum of Modern Art, 2018), demonstrates.

And on top of this lies the extraordinary phenomenon of what has come to be known as 'neo-Victorianism', exemplified by the enormous success of Sarah Waters's *Tipping the Velvet* (2002), and *Fingersmith* (2005), or the popularity of Sherlock Holmes reinterpretations or the stylized Victorian violence of the BBC/ Amazon Prime's *Ripper Street* (2012–16). There is nothing unusual in literature engaging with history, but the later 20th and 21st centuries have invested in an especially powerful way in the interpenetrations of the Victorian past, the present, and the imagined future. William Gibson and Bruce Sterling's *The Difference Engine* (1990) and Neal Stephenson's *The Diamond Age* (1995) helped spawn a whole gothic steampunk subculture across not just fiction, film, and television but also comic books and videogames. In the Marvel Comics universe the character of

Mister Sinister as a Victorian Darwinist scientist was progressively articulated from his original appearance in the 1980s through to the 2010s, and the *Assassin's Creed* game series and films like the *League of Extraordinary Gentlemen* take advantage of the gaslit gothic aesthetics of Victorian London while trading on knowing reference to Charles Dickens, Florence Nightingale, Charles Darwin, and Alexander Graham Bell.

Perhaps understandably, critical approaches to neo-Victorian literature rarely dwell on concerns about its historical representativeness. Events like the 2019 Compass festival in Connecticut, with its 'Splendid Teapot Racing' event, open to anyone bringing a teapot on a remote-controlled chassis, alongside demonstrations of cane fighting and parasol defence, luxuriate in the unapologetic anachronism of steampunk. But by focusing attention on the ways in which the past might intrude into the present and shape the future, neo-Victorianism vividly affirms the ways the Victorians continue to haunt the contemporary consciousness.

Using the Victorians

The dazzling inventiveness of neo-Victorianism reminds us that the afterlife of the Victorians has always been as much a matter of usefulness as status, a reflection of the ease with which they can be appropriated and exploited. And indeed, throughout the 20th century the Victorians functioned as a strange hybrid of sounding board and Aunt Sally: not just in Britain, the Victorians remained the 20th century's cultural 'other', a context against which new generational identities were forged and new ways of thinking tempered, a space in which values could be challenged or affirmed, and evil could be both distanced and domesticated. Historical fictions of the Victorian have never entirely escaped from the pleasures of pointing out just how far the Victorians fell short of their own self-image and our subsequent achievement. Neo-Victorian literatures often seek to validate contested elements of contemporary culture by affirming their vibrancy and longevity against the cul de sac of Victorian values.

These strategies inflected attitudes towards the Victorians for much of the 20th century. In the years before and after the First World War vitriolic anti-Victorianism of the sort propounded by modernists like Wyndham Lewis and Ezra Pound was increasingly vocal, and the patrician sneers of Lytton Strachey and the Bloomsbury Group echoed at least superficially by T. S. Eliot and W. H. Auden sought to undermine Victorian influence rather than enshrine it. The foundational text of this attitude, Strachey's *Eminent Victorians* (1918), presented his four Victorians, Thomas Arnold, Florence Nightingale, Cardinal Manning, and General Gordon, not as the heroes of Victorian hagiography, but as drunkards, tyrants, humbugs, and charlatans. Anti-Victorianism became part of the small change of anglophone intellectual life, the period a soft option for satire, as in Auden's later description of it as the time when 'Crying went out and the cold bath came in | with drains, bananas, bicycles and tin'. Victorianism was also a foil for attempts to throw off prudery and sexual repression in the 1960s, as in John Fowles's *The French Lieutenant's Woman* (1969), or a frame for 21st-century reappraisals of colonialism as represented by Matthew Kneale's *English Passengers* (2000) or Eleanor Catton's *The Luminaries* (2013).

At the same time, the 20th-century reaction against the Victorians always had its counterpoint in figures who looked back fondly on the certainties and social stability of the Victorians in comparison with the vulgarity and atomism of inter-war Britain. It would be easy to dismiss this as rather shallow nostalgia. And no doubt there was a powerful current of wistfulness. The Second World War imbued the Victorian era with a new allure. The public was suddenly, as the critic Basil Willey put it, 'yearning nostalgically after it.... In that distant mountain country all that we now lack seems present in abundance: not only peace, prosperity, plenty and freedom, but faith, purpose and buoyancy.' The enormous popularity of *Kilvert's Diary*, the journal of an obscure Victorian clergyman, published in 1941, suggests that in a period of industrial decline and international eclipse, the Victorians, ruling the waves and overseeing an empire on which the sun never set, were suddenly more attractive company.

In more recent decades versions of the Victorians have tended to combine both approaches, offering the opportunity to revel in our modern superiorities while cultivating a sneaking envy for the privileges and simplicities of the Victorians, who emerge as materialist but enterprising, complacent but secure, inclined to hypocrisy but at least able to believe. In the late 1990s the British Labour cabinet minister Roy Hattersley paid testimony to the instructive escapism offered by a volume such as Asa Briggs's *Victorian People*, confessing that 'When, during previous Christmasses, joy to all men has become too much to bear, I have regularly slipped away to the lavatory with Robert Lowe, Anthony Trollope, John Bright and Arthur Roebuck.'

It is a short step from nostalgia to deference, or at least a belief that the Victorians still have much to teach us. From H. W. Massingham's *The Great Victorians* (1932) to Dinah Birch's *Our Victorian Education* (2008) the Victorians have also been framed as the first moderns, wrestling—often successfully—with the same kinds of problems facing 20th-century society, and so a source of useful ideals, attitudes, and philosophies of practical assistance, as a way of obtaining 'courage and refreshment'. And a 21st-century justification of Victorian literature like Philip Davis's *Why Victorian Literature Still Matters* (2008) offers a different but equally nutritive sense of the importance of the Victorians and their literature: that they provide assumptions which offer empowerment and a space to feel, that it is impossible, as Davis puts it, 'to do without what the Victorians stand for'.

The controversy which raged in Britain in the 1980s when Margaret Thatcher's Conservative Party urged a return to

'Victorian Values' was only the most infamous instance of this approach. Thatcher's determination to use the Victorians both as morally exemplary and as part of the 'great landmarks' of British history ensured that they occupied a central place in Britain's late-century school curriculum. In America, neo-liberalism readily drew on Victorian examples in critique of the social problems of permissive society. And although we might imagine that 40 years on few would look to the Victorians in this way, political leaders continue to proclaim Victorian heroes and inspirations, Theresa May paying homage to Joseph Chamberlain, Boris Johnson to Churchill, and even Barack Obama drawing inspiration for his central message of hope from the Victorian painting of that name by George Frederick Watts.

Implications

When so much is at stake there is a danger of inauthenticity, of making representations of the Victorians more self-serving than truth-serving. To be fair, popular presentations of the Victorian often show a scrupulous concern with 'accuracy' at the level of detail, a sense of the responsibility the present owes to the past, but at times there is little regard to truth in the reimagination of spirit or message, or as respects the underlying historicity of the past. This is certainly the case for film and television representations, all the more treacherous as a guide for their superficial realism. For example, the understandable imperatives of diverse casting which have gathered pace within the last few years tend to create an image of the past which while not absolutely dishonest gives a fundamentally misleading impression of the racial textures of Victorian society. The lampoon in Malcolm Bradbury's novella *Cuts* (1987), in which the film executive responds to an actor's questioning that Gladstone would actually appear naked before Victoria playing the ukulele by asserting that the 'fictionalised verity' he aims at takes real people and events, but is 'not slavishly bound to actual facts', offers a reflection of the priority often given by television executives and popular novelists to message over veracity.

The relationship between the contemporary climate crisis and Victorian environmentalism offers a case in point. Although in recent years several Victorians have been co-opted as pioneers of modern environmental campaigns, Victorian notions of the environment were primarily shaped by long-standing equations of nature with God's creation and the Victorians' 'green' consciousness was largely a function of literary anti-industrialism and anti-modernism. So, while they could be horrified at the desecration wrought by a new railway, Victorians were largely unmoved by the way in which British globalism ravaged forests in New Brunswick, depleted soils in the American south, and exterminated carnivores in India and Africa. The Victorians provide little useful guidance in responding to these issues. Despite occasional interventions like W. H. Hudson's *The Purple Land that England Lost* (1885), or the cultural critic John Ruskin's *The Storm Cloud of the Nineteenth Century* (1884), the Victorians' emphasis was generally on the sort of local landscape preservation championed by Hardwicke Rawnsley and the National Trust, or an anxiety about resource exhaustion, rather than the sorts of global sustainability concerns which emerged in the 20th century. Instead of seeking self-validation through demonstrating the length of the history of ecocritical sensibilities, or searching for Victorian values and expressions which might be serviceable in the contemporary moment, ideals such as Ruskin's 'There is no wealth but life', we might better understand the Victorian 'greens' by accepting them on their own terms.

The danger in approaching the Victorians through the lens of our own preoccupations like this is that we isolate, we decontextualize, we over-interpret, we pay insufficient attention to circulation, readership, or influence, and in doing so, we make the Victorians appear a great deal more like us than they actually were.

The Victorians offer a standing risk of this sort of unwarranted familiarity. The adaptations of the *Forsyte Saga* by the BBC (1967) and ITV/PBS (2002–3) both offered a subtle canvas of contradictory forces and tendencies, but television adaptors and film directors regularly succumb to the temptation to make Victorian characters in the image of their contemporary equivalents. Despite the factories, the global reach, the suburbs, and the sewers, we are not living in the Victorian period. Despite the illusion of empathy, the Victorians were not just like us. To understand the Victorians requires awareness (and indeed wariness) of these differences: of the powerful pull of religious belief, not least on those who most stridently repudiated it; of precarity and the spectre of absolute poverty; of the casual racism founded on distance and contempt rather than closeness and a sense of threat; of a social mobility in which hierarchies of caste and class were difficult to shake off and wealth rarely decisive. We need to consider the implications of a society without cars and planes, radio and television, recorded music and the internet, where branded food and world cuisines, domestic showers, electrical appliances, old age pensions, and paperbacks were all largely unheard of.

Debates over 'cancel culture' are at one level a symptom of the challenge of managing not only the presence but also the distance of the past, and of the entanglements of memory and honour. Each historical moment must decide for itself which achievements and which attitudes it wishes to celebrate and which to condemn, while accepting that its standards are as transient and of the moment as those it judges. The arguments against commemorating Cecil Rhodes's violent and exploitative imperialism or the sexism of many Darwinists' belief in female biological inferiority are unanswerable. The moral reckoning of the often-hidden sources of individual and collective wealth is a necessary part of uncovering both realities and legacies of the past which are often occluded. But care is needed. If contemporary uses should be governed by contemporary values, historical understanding is rarely achieved by the desire to apportion guilt. That a Darwin or a Huxley shared some of the common prejudices of their period should not prevent us from celebrating their intellectual achievements (while distancing ourselves from those prejudices). It certainly cannot prevent us from recognizing their historical importance, just as the significance Mary Seacole has for our own perspective on the past should not disguise her relative insignificance to her contemporaries. We can judge our Victorian heritage from the standpoint of the present, but we can only understand Victorian history from the perspective of the past.

Writing the Victorians

That each era composes its own version of the past is a truism especially apposite for the Victorians, because their continued presence has inevitably prompted conflicts of possession, and the resulting rollercoaster reputation makes writings about the period a particularly treacherous terrain. Many of the 'classic' studies of the Victorians, including George Malcolm Young's *Victorian England: Portrait of an Age* (1936), Walter Houghton's *The Victorian Frame of Mind* (1957), and George Kitson Clark's *The Making of Victorian England* (1965), which all carry the illusion of currency because of the frequency with which they have been repackaged and republished, were an intervention in the debates of their day over the reputation of the Victorians as much as they were dispassionate histories, and they need to be read with this in mind.

More recently university historians have been reluctant to address the Victorians as an appropriate object of general interpretation, except perhaps in the sort of student-oriented texts of which Susie Steinbach's *Understanding the Victorians* (2016) and David Gange's *The Victorians: A Beginner's Guide* (2016) are the best examples. It has most often been literary scholars, of whom Richard Altick and Robin Gilmour stand out, who have produced broad academically rigorous interpretative surveys of the period.

Tellingly, none of the multi-volume histories of Britain of the last 40 years have chosen to take the Victorian period, or even some loose approximation to it, for the scope of a volume. Theodore Hoppen's *The Mid-Victorian Generation* for the Oxford History of Britain comes closest, but even this covers only the central two-thirds, from 1846 to 1886. In part these vagaries are just a consequence of editorial fiat or a reflection of the general fear that reifying any period distorts and fragments the continuities and complexities of history. But they also reflect a specific suspicion and at times disdain of the claims of the 'Victorian' as a period or category, of the sort intimated by the observation of the American cultural historian Morse Peckham that 'If we think that there once actually existed "Victorian culture" we shall for ever be hopelessly confused.'

Seeking to avoid the dangers of datedness drives readers to the steady stream of more ambitious syntheses for the general reader, including A. N. Wilson's *The Victorians* (2002), Simon Heffer's *High Minds: The Victorians and the Birth of the Modern* (2013), and innumerable television-series spin-offs like Jeremy Paxman's *The Victorians* (2009). Inevitably, some of these are stronger than others. Despite a substantial cargo of detail, they often reveal more about the idiosyncrasies of the authors than of the Victorians. Even when they escape from the unrelenting rhetoric of relevance, more recent popular studies often offer a view of the Victorians which reinforces the privileging in contemporary culture of personal characteristics and individual stories over general contexts and collective experiences, emphasizing ideas and perceptions over action and reality.

Conclusion

The controversies over Rhodes and the apparently insatiable public demand for the Victorians across all media show that as the 21st century has progressed the implications of the Victorians have become no less urgent, even if as each year passes the

1. Hew Locke, *Foreign Exchange* (Birmingham, 2022).

intimacy of our connection to them weakens. The appearance of Jacob Rees-Mogg's *The Victorians: Twelve Titans Who Forged Britain* in 2019 with its portentous moralizing, and of Hew Locke's reimagining of the city's statue of Queen Victoria in his *Foreign Exchange* installation for the Birmingham 2022 Festival, make clear that it would still be premature to assume that the Victorians have finally been safely consigned to history (Figure 1).

We should be clear about what we want from the Victorians and careful that our sense of them does not become whatever is most serviceable to us; that, for example, we emphasize their doubt because we have embraced our own, or condemn their certitudes because we have lost ours. We should be wary of the extremes both of nostalgia and of moral outrage. Above all, it will help in understanding the Victorians if we keep the different contexts, the tensions, and complexities of Victorian Britain in play: the conjunctions of change and continuity, ambition and complacency, conformity and division.

Chapter 3
The Victorian as period

When exactly was the Victorian period? And what does it mean to think of it as a historical 'period'?

For an era possessed of a literary canon, famous 'greats', and even its own '-ism', the limits adopted for the Victorian period have been remarkably flexible. Formally Victoria acceded to the throne on 20 June 1837 and reigned until her death on 22 January 1901. Although unfashionable, treating the years between these dates as a discrete period is not as ridiculous as it might at first seem. Victoria did have a historical influence in her own right. Her accession brought a change of mood, a sense of a break with the Hanoverian monarchy of the long 18th century; and her longevity eventually encouraged contemporaries to think of themselves as Victorians, living in an 'age' defined by the Queen. We should not underestimate both Victoria's active involvement in government decisions, and the cultural glue she provided, embodied in the proliferation of images, the statues, the Victoria Halls and Victoria Parks. Republicanism was insignificant; the Victorians were instinctively monarchist.

The Queen read the official papers and met regularly with her prime ministers to tell them her thoughts and wishes, and where the standing of the monarchy was particularly touched, as in respect to her elevation to Empress of India in 1876, her wishes were even more important. A conservative by temperament, someone whose attitudes and sensibilities progressed little from adolescence, H. G. Wells's description of her as 'a giant paperweight that for half a century sat upon men's minds' was only partly unfair. It was no accident that Lytton Strachey's Bloomsbury counterblast against the Victorians progressed from his *Eminent Victorians* to the Queen as a supplementary target of his corrosive invective.

But as the influence of the monarchy declined the regnal dates of kings and queens have diminishing relevance for national history, and so, for all the contemporary acknowledgement of her importance, scholars have generally been reluctant to take the notion of a unitary Victorian period seriously. It is suggested that the apparent coherence given by Victoria's longevity is at best spurious, and at worst positively debilitating, constraining history within unhelpful boundaries and even hobbling these years with a gendered identity which has fed into the negative stereotypes of Victorianism. The literary historian John Lucas maintained that 'except in the most rigorously controlled of contexts, "Victorian" and "Victorianism" are terms we could well do without. They are all too frequently employed in ways that are chronologically indefensible, historically dubious, intellectually confusing, and ideologically unacceptable.'

Part of the problem has been the lack of any real consensus about what we mean when we say that there was a 'Victorian period', and in suggesting here that there was one, we should clear up some potential misapprehensions. Defending the idea of a Victorian period does not mean slavishly insisting on the specific importance of 1837 or 1901. Nor does it imply that the beginnings and ends of the Victorian years were marked by a revolutionary historical rupture which effectively broke connections with what came before or after. Neither does it suggest any sort of unchangeableness or stasis across the 60 years, especially as regards ideology or 'zeitgeist' (that invaluable German word which is used to indicate the 'world view' of a period or collective).

We might as easily say the reverse is true. Britain in 1895 was in many, perhaps in most, respects quite different from the Britain of 1840. The reign was punctuated with important moments of change, not least in the national mood or the tone of public life, moments which require us to think of it as comprising several distinct sub-periods. Nonetheless the start and end of the reign did coincide with moments of wide-ranging transformation, even if only roughly, and there were powerful persistences and continuities across the intervening period. Where change occurred during the Victorian years, it often did so within consistent vectors of development, lines laid down in the early years and progressively worked through.

The rest of this chapter aims to provide an outline of the chronological pattern which resulted, and tries to give a sense of the structure of the period. My argument is that the nature and timings of the major historical watersheds of the 1830s and the years around 1900, and of the less dramatic but still important transitions which occurred between these two moments, effectively create a series of sub-periods.

Traditionally, historical surveys talk of early, mid-, and late Victorian Britain. With respect to the first, it is widely accepted that the years 1848–51 saw a meaningful change, ushering in the mid-Victorian years. Conventionally the mid-Victorian period is presented as coming to an end in the years 1867–70. The problem with this approach is that it leaves a final late Victorian period which is as long as the first two periods combined and lacks their coherent character. At times a solution has been sought by pushing the end of the mid-Victorian years on to the mid-1870s or even 1880. But there is no obvious divide in the mid-1870s, and a better solution is to acknowledge that the important events of the mid-1880s amount to a further inflection point, creating not three but four sub-periods, early, mid-, and (from around 1885) late Victorian, and also what we might describe as the 'high Victorian' period from the late 1860s to the mid-1880s. As we shall see, each of these has their distinct identity while sharing in the underlying character of the period as a whole which is explored further in the next chapter.

Opening

In truth, 1837 was a rather nondescript year to serve as the start of a momentous period in British history. It marked less a point of departure than the culmination of a period of intense and widespread change. At best it offered portents, signs of the times which can be read retrospectively. So, the start of a new reign required a general election which saw one Benjamin Disraeli elected to parliament for the first time. The first steamship designed for crossing the Atlantic, the SS *Great Western*, was launched and the patent on which the first commercial telegraph operated was granted. The publication of Thomas Carlyle's *French Revolution* set the tone for a period haunted by the fear of revolution, while the first serial issues of Dickens's *Oliver Twist* announced the arrival of a new literature. But these are merely straws in the wind.

The year 1832, on the other hand, offers a much more convincing starting point for a Victorian period. Agricultural unrest and the agitation for reform made this a year of profound crisis. The 'Great' Parliamentary Reform Act which emerged was in many respects a limited and conservative measure, leaving most of the adult population without a vote, and the aristocratic elites entrenched in control. But its significance lay less in the numbers than in the sense of modernization it mobilized. Politics was opened up. The most egregious examples of 'rotten boroughs' with tiny electorates were removed, and the representation of expanding towns and cities was enhanced. And most importantly, a hotchpotch of eligibilities to vote based on accidents of custom and tradition was replaced by just two parallel urban and rural franchises each based on deliberate calculations of individual fitness. Quite suddenly, the politics of the 1810s seemed part of a distant past. Sir James Mackintosh, the Whig law reformer, reflecting on the changes, suggested that it was as if he had 'lived in two different countries and conversed with people who spoke different languages'.

And this was just the start. By ushering in almost continuous Whig government from 1832 to 1841 the Act made the 1830s a pivotal decade of reform, a word now much more frequently and approvingly invoked. Mackintosh's remarks reflected the wider transformation which took place with notable rapidity in the middle years of the 1830s, a transformation which in many respects marked the end of Britain's *ancien régime*. The 18th-century legal system, based on the 'bloody code' of savage intimidatory sentencing, was dismantled, leading amongst other things to a rapid decline in the use of the death penalty. The remnants of the political repression introduced during and immediately after the Napoleonic wars were relaxed. The evils of unrestricted industrial working hours were addressed, albeit only in part, by factory legislation. The position of the Church of England as in effect an executive arm of the state was dramatically loosened, and the self-serving and often self-nominating closed municipal corporations which had ruled many of the country's towns were reformed to allow greater popular control and efficiency.

One of the ironies of these measures is that they occurred largely independently of social and economic change. It was once the historical orthodoxy that the political reforms of the 1830s were responses to a sudden and dramatic 'industrial revolution' and the rise of a new middle class, but nowadays it is recognized that the economic and social change of the early 19th century, although enormous, was also both gradual and uneven, characterized by the coexistence of old handicrafts and the new industries, and the survival of established forms of paternalism and deference alongside new class divisions brought about by the replacement of relationships of mutual social obligation with transactions confined to the 'cash nexus' of wages. Even so, there can be no doubt that in important respects the 1830s did see the acceleration of a series of changes which had been creating a radically different 'industrial society', and that this, and in particular the urban forms and problems which it produced, became suddenly and intensely visible at this moment. In many respects Victorian culture was shaped henceforth by its confused and often contradictory attempts to make sense of this new urban world.

Early Victorian challenge

Central to this awareness was a preoccupation with what came to be known as the 'Condition of England question'. Despite its continued growth, early Victorian Britain was a period of particularly sustained economic hardship and intense social conflict. Rapid and largely uncontrolled urban development would have inevitably brought challenges of sanitation and pollution, especially given the rudimentary contemporary understandings of the causes of disease. These were compounded by the overcrowding and deterioration caused by the failure of housing supply to keep pace with urban population growth, and by a violent cycle of economic booms and slumps which produced periodic episodes of large-scale unemployment.

For sanitary reformers, urban investigators, and social novelists the dislocations of the 'Hungry Forties' encouraged a diagnosis of societal malaise rooted in an imagined deformation of the working-class home and family life. In contrast, the groups bearing the brunt of the hardship blamed their position on their political and economic impotence and mounted a sustained challenge to the parliamentary settlements of the early 1830s, with an ambition and appeal and a revolutionary undertone which distinguished their actions from the radicalism of the 1810s and 1820s. Ebbing and flowing between peaks of activity in 1839, 1842, and 1848, the Chartist movement along with campaigns for Poor Law reform and factory legislation created a sense of social and political insecurity which only finally waned after 1848.

The success with which the ruling classes contained the challenges of radicalism owed much to the ways in which the political system adjusted to the new circumstances. In parliament executive control was strengthened. Reforms of taxation, of the banking system, and ultimately of the policies of protectionism (especially the Corn Laws) which had kept food prices artificially high since the Napoleonic wars allowed governing elites to project the social and economic impartiality of the state, absolving it of direct economic responsibility, dissociating it from social disputes, and emphasizing its commitment to ensuring the efficient working of the free market. Information-gathering bureaucracies expanded significantly: the central registration of births, marriages, and deaths via the General Register Office set up in 1837, the first comprehensive census in 1841, and the rapid intensification of parliamentary investigations together transformed the ways in which ordinary people came within the purview of the state. Even so, central government remained tiny, and the working through of the adjustments of the 1830s was more visible in local government. Institutions of local administration were steadily rationalized. Reformed municipal corporations, Boards of Guardians, county prisons, and local police forces, an explosion of voluntary associations, and the diminished role of parish vestries, all made the early Victorian period a new golden age of local action.

For all the weakening of organized religion's civil power, these years were also ones of religious revival, precipitated by the 'Oxford movement', a diffuse but powerful call to the Church of England to restore the purity of the early Church, launched by

John Keble's sermon on 'National Apostasy' in 1833, and articulated in a series of 'Tracts for the Times' published between 1833 and 1841. The response which this call prompted within Anglicanism, and the reaction of Nonconformity to the re-energized Church, gave early Victorian Britain a particularly warm interdenominational rivalry, played out both in the rush to build churches and chapels to provide for the 'unchurched masses', and then in the intractable disputes over how to enlist government support in the provision of education for the working classes.

Mid-Victorian equipoise

Towards the end of the 1840s the challenges of the early Victorian period began to wane. The change was signalled first by the repeal of the Corn Laws in 1846 and the subsequent break-up of the Conservative Party of Sir Robert Peel, quickly followed by the decisive defeat of Chartist agitation in 1848. Although formally Chartism limped on into the 1850s, the melting away of the Chartists' revolutionary menace at the mass Kennington Common demonstration in April 1848 left the movement in tatters and its leadership in disgrace. This dodging of the revolutions which wracked the Continent in the same year appeared to vindicate the moderate reforms of the previous 15 years. The events of 1848 also cemented the personal popularity of Lord Palmerston, insulating him from his critics, and paving the way for his dominance of politics until his death in 1865. The failure of Victoria's attempt to dismiss Palmerston in 1851 demonstrated how irreplaceable he had become.

By this point the passing of the 'Hungry Forties' had been given powerful symbolic affirmation by the Great Exhibition and its remarkable Crystal Palace of iron and glass, which over the course of four months in 1851 attracted over 6 million visitors from across Britain and the world. The Exhibition reassured the Victorians of their dominance of the global economy. It reinforced the significance of the monarchy in the guise of Victoria's husband

Prince Albert, and the sight of millions of well-behaved working-class visitors confirmed the lessons that observers had already drawn from 1848 about the essential stability of British society. Looking back from 1914, the jurist A. V. Dicey, who was 16 at the time, claimed the Exhibition 'had a significance which is hardly understood by the present generation...The ideas of the political economists, and above all the dogma of *laissez-faire*, had...achieved a final victory.'

The Great Exhibition symbolized a new period of balance between progressive and regressive forces, between Conservative and Liberal, Anglican and Nonconformist. Certainly the years after 1851 were much less fraught than those before 1848. The repeal of the Corn Laws and subsequent further reductions in tariffs in 1849 not only helped to bring a new and more widely shared economic prosperity, but also undercut the long-standing critique of the state as a vehicle of aristocratic self-enrichment. Agriculture shrugged off the ending of protection; industry leapt forwards, and the value of British trade grew substantially. Income from overseas investments quadrupled between 1851 and 1871. Despite periodic reverses, the demand for labour became more buoyant. Real wages improved, slowly but significantly.

We should not overdo the point. The evidence of economic progress in the 1850s and 1860s is uneven at best. The economy was still prone to crises; the one in 1857–8 was particularly acute. Many of the working classes continued to have very little disposable income. Urban conditions remained stubbornly resistant to improvement, but employer paternalism, the extension of philanthropy, and the growth of associations of mutual support such as building societies and the cooperative movement all dulled the force of social conflict. The skilled working class turned to new forms of trades unionism, and working-class radicalism ceased to be a meaningful threat. Middle-class radicalism too lost its edge and turned towards more ameliorist action, especially in education and recreation. The old

Chartist Thomas Cooper looked on in disgust at well-dressed working men preoccupied with cooperative store dividends and building society shares.

This was the 'age of Palmerston'. His mix of caution at home and bluster abroad was anathema to the radicals in his party, but it caught the mood of greater confidence and assertiveness in the country as a whole. In politics, Liberalism was the dominant force; the split in the Conservative Party in 1846 between the followers of Peel and the rest of the Conservatives ushered in a period in which it failed to win six successive general elections, and until 1868 its only experiences of government were brief minority administrations. This was a time of fluidity with little in the way of major policy divides, which made parliament rather than the electorate the decisive forum for the making and unmaking of governments. Characteristically modest reforms like the abolition of the 'taxes on knowledge' encouraged the expansion of the cheap (and Liberal) press, while in a succession of budgets W. E. Gladstone implemented the ideals of cheap government and free trade espoused in Mill's *Principles of Political Economy* (1848). At the same time, Palmerston pursued a more belligerent foreign policy which led Britain into the only European war it fought during the reign, the Crimean War with Russia between 1853 and 1856, quickly followed by the reign's most harrowing imperial conflict, a rebellion traditionally known as the Indian 'Mutiny' of 1857.

In the 20th century the mid-Victorian years acquired a reputation for smugness and complacency. This was never entirely fair. Beneath the superficial serenity, it was a period of powerfully conflicting forces which just happened to largely cancel each other out in a moment of equipoise. But the ebbing sense of crisis did encourage the consolidation of middle-class orthodoxies. The 1857 Manchester Art Treasures Exhibition and the Leeds Town Hall (1853–8) manifested the cultural confidence of the industrial middle classes. A new consensus emerged around elements of

Victorian individualism and classical political economy which had struggled to gain general assent in the 1840s. It is telling that the 1850s saw the publication of many of the texts which would come to be seen as classic representations of the character of the whole period, especially Samuel Smiles's *Self Help* (1859). John Ruskin's essays and Coventry Patmore's *The Angel in the House* (1854–6) affirmed the gendered ideology of separate spheres. T. H. Buckle's *History of Civilization in England* (1857, 1861) expressed the new confidence in Britain's national progress and destiny. These were the years when Martin Tupper's *Proverbial Philosophy* and the sort of commonsense cultural conservatism it celebrated enjoyed the peak of its popularity, going through nearly 40 editions from 1850 to 1860. The cautious feminism of Barbara Bodichon and Emily Faithfull and the Langham Place group which flourished from the later 1850s to the mid-1860s, although a significant moment in the history of the women's movement, epitomized the limited ambition which seemed to characterize reform initiatives in the period.

High Victorian anxiety

As we move into the 1860s renewed signs of strain begin to emerge. Another of the publications of 1859, Charles Darwin's *On the Origin of Species*, set in motion the century's most important intellectual revolution, although one whose implications were really only fully felt after the publication of his *The Descent of Man* in 1871. The appearance soon after the publication of *Origin* of the volume *Essays and Reviews* (1860) placed traditional views of biblical authority and religious truth under further stress. The frenetic sensationalism which was a noticeable feature of the popular fiction of the decade also contributed to a fresh sense of cultural crisis. But it was the death of Palmerston in 1865 which precipitated a further moment of inflection. For the next 20 years Gladstone was the central figure in British public life and his duel with Disraeli was the primary axis of politics. Gladstone's support gave franchise reform fresh impetus, visible in the campaigns of the newly established Reform Union and Reform League. The sudden reappearance of civil disorder in the 1866 Hyde Park riots, a banking crisis, trade union violence, all followed by Fenian terrorism in the spring of 1867, brought a renewed fear of revolution, while Britain's dismal showing at the 1867 Paris International Exhibition cast doubt on the superiority that had been demonstrated in 1851. The growth of Prussian power manifest in Prussia's defeats of Austria in 1866 and France in 1870–1 fundamentally altered the balance of power and terms of engagement in Europe, just as the opening of the Suez Canal reinforced the strategic importance of the Middle East in the communications networks which bound the British empire together.

Contemporaries compared 1867 to 1848 as years of great significance. In many respects the Parliamentary Reform Act of the year was merely a further instalment of the widening franchise implicit in the 1832 settlement, involving a Disraelian sleight of hand in which the extended franchise granted to the boroughs was cancelled out by greater numbers of largely unreformed county seats, but this did not stop middle-class observers seeing it as a 'Leap in the Dark' towards greater political power for working-class voters. Perhaps more seismic in practice were the opportunities provided for the first time by the reforms in education and municipal government for unmarried women to vote and for women to be elected to serve on the newly established school boards.

These years between 1867 and the next moment of national crisis in the mid-1880s lack the obvious distinctiveness of the early and mid-Victorian periods, which helps to explain why they are frequently glossed over or annexed to the periods before or after. They don't obviously possess a separate literary character, although George Eliot's later novels, including *Middlemarch*, and the editorial tone of the most influential of the new serious monthly journals, the *Fortnightly Review* under John Morley, were clearly a reflection of what Kathryn Hughes has described as the 'anxious and high-minded 1870s'. The years after 1867 also encompassed a shift to disciplinary specialism and greater academic authority, presaged by the launch of *Nature* in 1869, and coincided with the life of the Metaphysical Society, which from 1869 to its collapse in 1880 sought to provide a forum where intellectuals of all persuasions and backgrounds might establish common ground in the fierce debates over the relations of science and religion.

The fear that the unrest of the later 1860s might presage a more general collapse of social order loomed large. In the wake of the troubled ruminations of the liberal intellectual Matthew Arnold in his *Culture and Anarchy* (1869), anxiety and disquiet at the implications of the march of democracy became a feature of political commentary, visible in texts such as Fitzjames Stephen's *Liberty, Equality, Fraternity* (1873), and in Ruskin's two long-running critiques of middle-class culture, *Fors Clavigera* (1871–84) and *Proserpina* (1875–86). Arnold's horror at the influence of what he described as 'Hebraism', by which he meant what he saw as the harsh, Old Testament-infused, culturally repressive puritanism of Victorian Nonconformity, was a response to the shift in provincial leadership at the end of the 1860s from Manchester, with its broad Unitarian and non-denominational radicalism, to the more militantly Nonconformist Birmingham, where local Liberals championed the educational interests of Dissent and the politics of the local party caucus.

Despite the Conservatives being briefly in power during the passing of the 1867 Reform Act, the Liberals remained in office for 12 of the 18 years between 1868 and 1885. Even with the expanded electorate there was no sudden shift towards collectivism or pressure for more interventionist government. But a greater role for the state in pursuit of the common good was much more apparent in the new liberalism emerging around 1870 in the writings of the influential Oxford philosopher T. H. Green. More conservative Liberals looked on with mounting unease at the rise of programmatic politics which seemed to be manifest in Gladstone's 'Midlothian campaign' of 1879–80, worried that politics had become increasingly about pandering to sectional self-interests rather than the pursuit of the common good.

Agrarian unrest fed the growth of Irish nationalism which pushed the question of Ireland into the centre of British politics, where it remained for the rest of the reign. In the 1870s the policy of Gladstonian liberalism was to 'pacify' Ireland through remedial reforms of the Church of Ireland and tenant rights. The election in 1885 of 86 Irish Nationalist MPs demonstrated the bankruptcy of this approach. Nor did Gladstonian Liberalism ever entirely cement its alliance with the 'Nonconformist conscience'. Universities opened up, state education was expanded (expenditure in London tripled between 1870 and 1885); but in education and temperance Liberal reforms fell well short of meeting Nonconformist aspirations. Josephine Butler's campaigns against the Contagious Diseases Acts of the 1860s, which had seemed to introduce state-sanctioned prostitution, campaigns sustained until their repeal in 1885, put both Liberals and Conservatives on the defensive.

The publication of W. S. Jevons's *The Theory of Political Economy* (1871) helped prompt a widespread crisis of confidence in classical economics, just as doubts were coalescing about Britain's economic superiority. Although London's position as the dominant global capital market was reinforced by the defeat of France in 1871 and the flight to Britain of many European financiers, the perception grew that Britain was losing its technological advantage and its industrial dominance. Ironically, it was finally in these years that urban working-class living standards began visibly to improve: from 1861 to 1881 average real wages grew by over a third. The nutritional level of British diets steadily improved and rising discretionary spend helped fuel the emergence of new forms of commercial leisure, including spectator sports. But the countryside told a different tale. In the 1870s and 1880s Britain was drawn further into a global agrarian system in which first American wheat and then chilled and frozen meat imports undercut British production, threatened landed wealth, and led to an absolute decline in the rural population for the first time.

Late Victorian revolt

Of all the reign's turning points the middle years of the 1880s probably offer the most clearly defined and decisive watershed. So much so that it is often suggested that the period after 1885 is best understood as 'post-Victorian'. The sense of strain and dislocation felt by contemporaries, encapsulated in the disillusionment Tennyson expressed in his 'Locksley Hall Sixty Years After' (1886), and W. H. Mallock's *The Old Order Changeth*, published in the same year, was the outcome of a convergence of numerous forces. These years saw another of the period's short-term economic crises and another bout of political reform, this time not just a further extension of the franchise, but also a redrawing of the constituency map which finally removed the distinction between rural and urban seats and gave the large centres of English population their full electoral due for the first time. For the Birmingham industrialist Joseph Chamberlain the consequences were clear: 'The centre of power has been shifted, and the old order is giving place to the new.'

Perhaps even more important than the parliamentary reforms of the 1880s in laying the foundations of the changed character of late Victorian government and politics was the decision of Gladstone to endorse Home Rule for Ireland. The Liberal Home Rule bill in 1886 marked the end of his attempts to pacify Ireland by reform of land rights, and precipitated the break-up of the Liberal Party, the ensuing 15 years witnessing the slow but steady migration of the 'Liberal Unionists' to Conservatism. Economic tensions re-energized labour politics; although the modern

Labour Party was a creation of the post-Victorian period, the formation in 1893 of the Independent Labour Party demonstrated that the momentum was towards autonomous representation for the working classes, as well as highlighting the implications of an ever-widening franchise, which brought significant investments from both Liberals and Conservatives in new forms of political organization, most notably the elaborate Primrose League, through which the Conservatives sought to build a broad electoral base by exploiting popular deference and patriotism.

Britain continued to lose its price competitiveness during the 1880s and 1890s, with a particularly sharp decline in the early 1890s. While Britain like the rest of Europe went through a 'second industrial revolution' in which coal, iron, and textiles were supplemented by light engineering, and an extended range of machine-made articles and mass produced commodities—think bicycles, biscuits, and machine-made boots—it was clear that its foreign industrial rivals were more successfully exploiting the new opportunities. Family businesses converted defensively into limited liability companies; small firms merged into larger and hopefully more resilient ones. The industrial middle classes saw themselves edged aside by a new plutocracy of city financiers and imperial adventurers. Inspired by high-profile disputes in the docks and by the Bryant and May matchgirls, trades union membership almost tripled between 1886 and 1901. The decision not to protect agriculture from cheap American wheat brought on a crisis in the arable counties, paralleled by 'Land war' in Ireland and crofters' conflicts in the Scottish Highlands. The final decade of the reign, like the first, saw technological change bring structural unemployment and industrial strife, and with it a return of the 'condition of England' question, now, as a result of Andrew Mearns's *Bitter Cry of Outcast London* (1883) and the notoriety of the Jack the Ripper murders in Whitehall in 1888, focused on the East End of London. There was a fresh flurry of Royal Commissions, on Housing, Labour, and the Aged Poor, and a new sensibility in which the problem of overcrowding replaced concerns about sanitation.

With British manufacturing visibly lagging behind its European neighbours, the fear of competition helped to promote Germany into the position of foremost international rival. Grumblings about the dangers of free trade began to be heard. Empire suddenly acquired a new importance. The Berlin Congress of 1884–5, in which the European powers sought to reconcile their competing desires for empire, refocused imperial policy towards pre-emptive action, setting in motion the 'scramble for Africa'. In the wake of the Colonial and Indian Exhibition of 1886, Victorian culture went imperial. The empire was imagined as a coherent unity for the first time. Military metaphors proliferated and military values acquired a new lustre; membership of the officer corps became de rigueur at the public schools. The trend was for missionary exhibitions, emigration-promotion societies, imperialist adventure yarns, a celebration of conquest and looting which the anti-imperialist J. A. Hobson described as the 'spectatorial lust' of late Victorian popular imperialism.

For commentators like the critic Holbrook Jackson, the 1890s became 'naughty', a little narcissistic, and desperate for novelty. But we must be careful not to give too much weight to a narrow avant-garde elite. The treatment of Oscar Wilde, first feted and then vilified, showed that if the grip of orthodoxy slackened as the century ended, it did not let go. Contemporaries experienced the final years of Victoria's reign as the hollowing out rather than the overthrow of established patterns. Dominated by novelists such as Hall Caine and Marie Corelli, the literary market was more suburban than subversive, and it was not so much modernism as the mass market that seemed the main corrosive. Nevertheless, there can be little doubt that established patterns were being undercut. If evolution's theological threat was largely neutered by its absorption into well-established theologies of progress towards human perfection, social Darwinian and eugenic ideas, with their fear of hereditary indigence and criminality, offered a fundamental challenge to liberal progressivism. Debates over the 'new woman' successfully challenged long-standing gender stereotypes. The career of the Ladies Guides Association, established in 1888 to open up the West End to unchaperoned women, which folded in 1902 on the basis that its services were no longer really required, points to the chronological bounds of this transition. Looking back in 1919, with the catastrophe of the Great War still fresh to mind, the Liberal academic James Bryce felt that 'living in a new world, the change seems to me to have come almost entirely in the fifteen years between 1885 and 1900'.

Entering the Edwardian era

With perhaps one notable caveat, 1901 like 1837 was not a year of momentous events: 'there has been little to lead us to suppose', *The Times* commented at its end, 'that future historians will concern themselves very greatly with the year'. But even if changes in electoral law meant that the death of the monarch no longer automatically triggered a general election, Victoria's death was very widely acknowledged as momentous, a forerunner of huge changes. In *The Forsyte Saga* John Galsworthy conjured its impact in his description of the crowds watching the Queen's funeral procession: 'a murmuring groan from all the long line of those who watched...Tribute of an age to its own death...The Queen was dead, and the air of the greatest city upon earth grey with unshed tears.' Even his cynical hero Soames felt the Queen's death as 'supremely symbolical, this summing-up of a long rich period'.

Once again, change on the throne coincided with a number of other events and processes, and it was the interaction of the whole which justifies the demarcation of the years around 1901 as the end of a period. Most important was the Boer War. As the Queen died, Britain was in the throes of fighting in South Africa. Although popular memory has rightly been drawn to the 'Great

War' of 1914 to 1918, the effects of the conflicts in South Africa were also widespread and profound.

The struggle to impose Britain's will on a tiny population of Boers, and the brutal methods used, including concentration camps and scorched earth, prompted a fresh bout of introspection and national soul-searching. The war crystallized the threat posed by German ambition, paving the way for a reorientation of British diplomacy towards alignment with France and Russia. Differences over the war hardened the fracture of Victorian Liberalism, facilitated the breakthrough of the Labour Party, and reinstated protectionism as a viable policy for the first time since the mid-1840s. Britain's place in world trade changed dramatically in the ensuing decade: its share of coal exports, for example, fell from 85 per cent in 1900 to only 50 per cent in 1913. And the pressure that the cost of war placed on government expenditure was a material factor in the educational reforms clustered around the 1902 Education Act which dismantled almost entirely the Victorian system of central support for denominational education.

The transition from the 19th century to the 20th also by happenstance coincided with a number of significant technological and cultural changes, including the arrival of the radio age, the rapid proliferation of telephones, and of course the dramatic impact of the internal combustion engine and the sudden boom in both cars and buses. Edwardian literature and drama began to throw off the imperatives of moral purpose. Pleasure trumped piety. Reticence receded: wealth was flaunted with ever greater ostentation; something of the same could be said of sex. From the perspective of 1918 it was easy to see the Edwardian age as a time of froth and innocence rudely shattered by the catastrophe of modern warfare. But even before 1914 old Victorians had looked on appalled at a world which, as one put it, had 'lost much of the higher spirit which inspired our public and private life not more than thirty years ago', in which '[t]he reek of the pothouse, the music-hall, the turf, of the share-market, of the thieves' fence infects our literature, our manners our amusements and our ideals of life'.

Conclusion

The years of Victoria's reign were not stable, and the experiences of older and younger Victorians were far from identical. Indeed the existence of distinct sub-periods was quite clear to contemporaries, as was the immensity of some of the changes which had occurred across those lifetimes that had spanned the 1830s to the 1880s and 1890s. At the same time, a Victorian who fell asleep in 1845 to wake in 1895 would have found their new surroundings remarkably familiar: more railways, more newspapers, more churches and chapels, bigger towns and cities, but still the same forms and ideals, and much of the same preoccupations. It is to the nature of these continuities that the next chapter turns.

Chapter 4
Victorianism

Setting the scene

The challenge of seeing the Victorians in the round, in all their
contradictions and complexities, is not helped by the way the
Victorians have been persistently gaslit by their successors, who
have suggested that the period can be encapsulated not by a
narrative of its events, or a description of its conditions and
characteristic experiences, but by a set of norms and values,
conventional attitudes and behaviours which—it is implied—were
shared by everyone. There are more positive versions, but in
general 'Victorianism' has been used to weigh the Victorians down
with an enormous baggage of negative association: baby farming,
constricted clothing, smugness and misogyny, horror of sex,
over-ornamented interiors, and sentimental art. It was a reduction
offered by the earliest modernists, and it is a phantasmagoria
which has been conjured by critics ever since.

This has always been a questionable approach. In his *Portrait of
an Age* G. M. Young asserted that 'Victorianism was a myth',
remarking that the biggest challenge with the Victorians was
finding anything on which they agreed. The suggestion that all
Victorians shared a particular set of beliefs can only ever be a
gross oversimplification, although one for which the Victorians
must accept some responsibility, because the idea of the 'spirit of

the age' or the zeitgeist was one which they themselves willingly embraced. The weaknesses of the approach are no less important for being so very obvious. Traditional versions of 'Victorianism' take the attitudes and behaviours of a narrow section of the 19th-century evangelical middle class and suggest that they can be applied across the whole of the population and across the whole of the period. At best, this reduces a complex history to personality, privileging thinking over doing, and ideals over realities. At worst it leads to the sort of caricature that suggests the Victorians 'were not amused' or that they draped their chair legs to avoid any improper suggestion of female anatomy. It is hardly surprising then, even though recent descriptions remain far too ready to describe what 'the Victorians' believed or felt or valued, that historians have tended to look with scepticism on the use of 'Victorianism' as a shorthand for Victorian culture.

For all this, the idea survives, largely because it has proved useful in allowing the construction of a supposed orthodoxy against which all kinds of attitudes and activities can be celebrated as radical and subversive. So much so that 'Victorianism' at times seems to offer a mirror image of much that we would take as canonically 'Victorian', because most of the leading Victorian novelists, poets, critics, and sages offer a sort of reverse Victorianism, marshalling one set of conventional Victorian responses to attack another (in doing so ensuring the pervasiveness of preoccupations and approaches by the very act of assaulting them). The critique of sages from Carlyle to the socialist Edward Carpenter worked precisely because they simultaneously criticized and conformed to the values and conditions of their culture. Looking back in 1926 to his 1890 work *The New Spirit*, the sexologist Havelock Ellis confessed that his ability to 'toss [the Victorians] aside disdainfully' was rooted in the fact that he 'first absorbed all the fine essential juices they had to yield'; so that it was only 'the husks' that he was throwing away.

In this sense 'Victorianism', like all caricatures, contains at least a kernel of truth. But more important than its descriptive accuracy is its reflection of the society's prescriptive and potentially proscriptive pressures. The importance of the ideal is not disproved by its mismatch with reality. Convention mattered to the Victorians. Taboos were stark and powerful. Not least because the Victorians inhabited a society which preferred social over legal sanction, which was governed, as one observer put it, by 'fear of the social circle, fear of the newspaper, fear of being odd'. Working-class communities were no different, being disciplined by what one slum-dweller described as 'the detailed gossip of a closed society'. It was a culture unnerved by unorthodoxy, which valued conformity over individuality, cohesion over self-expression, which dealt in certainties and thought in black and white categories, a society in which social standing relied on character more than wealth or even antecedents, and where loss of reputation could have catastrophic consequences. The Victorians were prejudiced. They prejudged. They generalized. They inhabited a world of stereotypes: the graphic social personifications of *Punch*, the stock characters of stage and music hall, the cut-out heroes and villains of juvenile fiction.

Of course, conventions were influencers of behaviour rather than descriptions of it. But this does not detract from the force of public standards, and we should not treat capacity to disregard as implying the weakness or non-existence of the rules. The ideals were real and they had consequences. One of the characteristics of Victorian Britain was the strength of expectations and the potential significance of the results of (at least public) transgression. Social stigma was a powerful force, inducing an equally powerful self-discipline and self-censorship. Transgressors were often wracked with shame or the fear of being shamed. Loss of respectability could be disastrous. The fates of politicians Charles Parnell and Sir Charles Dilke in the 1880s, destroyed by divorce scandals, and of Oscar Wilde in the 1890s, shunned once his homosexuality became a matter of public conversation, and the recurrence of blackmail and revelatory secrets in Victorian fiction, speak to the enormous power of social expectation. As does the reverse: the purported failure of working-class families to live up to domestic ideals, which was deployed by reformers as a crucial argument for factory legislation or housing reform, or the denial of the franchise, while painters seeking to scandalize, and playwrights seeking to satirize, could achieve striking effect through the flouting of expectations.

Where they impinged on public policy, conventions were often enshrined in law or in state action. Take Sabbatarianism, for example. A proscription on non-religious activities on Sunday clearly derived from a narrow interpretation of the Bible which few outside the evangelical middle classes shared, but which retained powerful legal backing, vigorously if inconsistently enforced by police action. Only in 1896 was the opening of national museums and art galleries permitted by legislation. Obscenity laws periodically bore down on publishers of contraceptive advice or salacious foreign novels. But just as often considerations of morality were enforced not through legal sanction, but through the projection of the sorts of critical standards associated with mid-Victorian attacks on 'Fleshly poetry', or the avowed determination of the commercial circulating libraries, and above all Mudie's Library, to ensure that nothing of even the slightest 'questionable' character was dispensed by their branches into Victorian homes.

Conventions

Everyday life in Victorian Britain was governed by an elaborate framework of expectations and rules of behaviour, which if anything strengthened in the early decades of the period as much as a defence against social anonymity as a reflection of religious revival. At the same time, the insecurities of new wealth—not just for the middle classes, but also for the emerging 'labour aristocracy' of better-paid craft workers—encouraged the minute codification of social etiquette and created a buoyant market in conduct manuals or guides to domestic management, of which Isabella Beeton's *Mrs Beeton's Book of Household Management*, first published in 1861 and extended and reprinted until 1907, was only the most famous amongst hundreds. The gentry and the bulk of the working classes had no need to rely on published guides, but their expectations were equally defined, and for the socially ambitious there was the how-to guide *Enquire Within Upon Everything* (1856–) and its imitators.

Written or unwritten, rules ranged across all aspects of grooming, dress, and social interactions: the time and length of house calls, or the correct use of the working-class 'front parlour'. Take hats, for example, not just a sartorial marker of status, but also for all classes an index of right conduct. Wearing the right hat for the right occasion (and removing it at the right time) carried a significance it is hard for modern observers to appreciate. But it was reported that when Gladstone was hesitating in the 1880s over whether to raise Tennyson—poet laureate since 1850—to the peerage, his overriding anxiety was that Tennyson might insist on wearing the wrong sort of hat in the House of Lords.

The most powerful proscriptions operated around sex, and indeed all forms of relations between the sexes. This was the age of chastity and of the chaperone. Except for the very rich, extra-marital sexual activity was fatal to reputation. (In some working-class communities it was not uncommon for intercourse to commence before marriage, but generally this was only for already engaged couples.) Illegitimacy was an indelible stain, prostitution a moral poison. Unmarried mothers were hidden or ostracized, while a blind eye was turned to the philandering of men. Such codes were not new, but they did attain greater universality and force for the Victorians. The consequences of this can be seen in long-standing suspicions of the theatre and other forms of dramatic entertainment, in the

Victorianism

43

rejection of mechanical contraception, and in the fierce hostility to all forms of queer or gay behaviour.

It is here that the Victorians were most vulnerable to accusations of hypocrisy and double standards. Prudery in public coexisted with a juvenile smuttiness in private, and a façade of propriety often masked licentiousness. Statistics of prostitution, evidence of illegitimacy, innumerable personal accounts, all demonstrate how widely norms of sexual purity and marital monogamy were transgressed, and how much harder they bore down on women than on men. Legally adultery for a man was an accident, but for women it was always premeditated.

Sexual moralizing, later reinforced by Darwinian biology, fed into stereotypes of gender of the sort propagated by Coventry Patmore's narrative poem *The Angel in the House* (1854) and John Ruskin's lecture *Of Queen's Gardens* (1864). Gender identities tended to be framed as mutually opposed positions which stressed absolute difference. Putting the most favourable possible spin on these ideas, they promulgated a positive account of women's roles and responsibilities, as mothers, wives, and daughters, controlling the domestic spaces of home and family, and empowering a particular set of feminine virtues—nurturing, caring, consoling, reconciling—virtues which were exploited by early Victorian feminists to claim a wider sphere of activity for women outside the home in philanthropy, education, and eventually even in politics. But in practice, they authorized a picture of women as physically weak, irrational, and prone to hysteria, and with a paramount responsibility to bear and raise children, a picture used as a justification for denying women political rights, restricting their freedom to act in the public sphere, and ensuring wherever possible that they remained economically and legally subservient to fathers or husbands.

Ideals of masculinity were equally prescriptive but less restrictive. The shift from Georgian 'politeness' and manners to purpose and moral authenticity, from affect to action, brought a new emphasis on energy, assertiveness, emotional repression, independence, and authority over dependants, in ways that became increasingly muscular as the period progressed. The Victorian public sphere was male, as were Victorian definitions of citizenship. Such ideas were bourgeois in origin but classless in operation. In a fiercely competitive world a shared emphasis on the virtues of effort and self-reliance was hardly surprising, even if for the working classes it coexisted with a recognition of the benefits of mutualism and collective solidarities, and the extent to which they were at the mercy of forces often beyond the control of personal character.

Values

Gender prescriptions were expressed most systematically through ideals of the family, which G. M. Young described as one of the few vital articles of the 'common Victorian Faith'. Marriage and the family were inscribed with a range of meanings and functions, as the cement of society, as the bedrock of religious and moral training, as a place of refuge and restoration from the pressures of public life. Images such as Landseer's *Windsor Castle in Modern Times* (Figure 2) placed Victoria and her family at the heart of these ideals. Foreign visitors frequently commented on the Victorians' apparently unlimited appetite for commonplace celebrations of family life. *Punch*'s versions of domestic life, the Frenchman Hippolyte Taine observed, overwhelmingly dwelt on the charms and felicities of home. Spinsterhood was stigmatized, and family became a lens through which large parts of Victorian experience were filtered—as in the way Victorian art addressed war predominantly in terms of its impact on the family members left behind. Beyond the nuclear family, kinship ties were also remarkably powerful, a source of emotional and financial support, of patronage, of connection and repute. Much of the shock of Thomas Hardy's later novels (including *The Mayor of Casterbridge* and *Tess of the D'Urbervilles*) lay in the bitter challenge they offered to Victorian pieties of family.

2. Edwin Landseer, *Windsor Castle in Modern Times* (1841-3).

Idealization of family was inextricably entwined with the gospel of domesticity. 'Domophilia' was one of the characteristic *English Traits* identified by the American transcendentalist Ralph Waldo Emerson in the 1850s. The 'Home, sweet home' of popular song and increasingly ubiquitous domestic decorations was both a physical place and a symbolic space. Suburbanization and the decline of outworking widened the distance between living and working. The home was imagined as a place of refuge and succour. Of course, such niceties were inconceivable for the millions living in overcrowded terraces or cramped tenements, and the persistence with which investigators, charity workers, and municipal officials blamed the prevalence of poverty on the failure of the poor to live up to what was clearly a middle-class domestic ideal did much to perpetuate the estrangement of the classes and working-class suspicion of the state. Yet the working classes had always displayed their own versions of domesticity, and accounts of late Victorian and Edwardian life, not least Robert Robert's

The Classic Slum (1971), show how deeply ingrained these became as the period progressed.

At the heart of these fantasies of home and family was the idealized male breadwinner, providing for the needs of his family, an image itself the focal point of a bundle of values, of work, autonomy, self-reliance, and control. Providing for dependants was the fundamental responsibility of Victorian men. Economic success and failure were imbued with moral significance: poverty was a sign of deficiency of character, unemployment unmanly. For William Landels in his *How Men Are Made* (1859), 'It is by work, work, work,—constant and never ceasing work—work well and faithfully done…that you are to rise out of things into men.' As Ford Madox Brown's famous painting *Work* (1852–65) affirmed, labour had become noble, an aspiration for all classes. 'We are all workers' became one of the most tired clichés of a culture not short of candidates for the accolade.

The elevation of work led on to other virtues, of the sorts celebrated by Thomas Carlyle and Samuel Smiles: perseverance, patience, industry, thrift, moderation, improvement, and above all self-help, each of which in turn threw out their own further articulations, thrift leading to temperance, the avoidance of borrowing, and the value of saving. Smiles's most widely read volume, *Self-Help* (1859), based on lectures delivered in the 1840s, was only one in a series of exhortatory texts which he sold widely in the following 30 years, including *Character* (1872) and *Thrift* (1876), and Smiles himself was only the most enduring of an army of sermonizers and moralists amongst whom Martin Tupper and his *Proverbial Philosophy* (1838–) seemed for the first half of the period to be particularly successful in catching the Victorian mood.

Tupper's compendium of aphorisms masquerading as ideology cast a baneful shadow, converting social issues into moral problems, reinforcing emphasis on the reform of individuals rather than institutions. Such ideas had their political expression in the preference for small government and for local mutualism rather than state intervention; but also in the principle of 'less eligibility' (the intention that the experience of inmates in the workhouses should be less attractive than the most impoverished of those able to continue to live without state support) at the heart of the poor law regime introduced in 1834, which under the guise of avoiding incentives to idleness punished pauperism as a failure of character. But it is easy to forget that Smiles started out as a radical and that his ideas championed personal growth and communal progress, producing a reformist frame of mind which instigated a myriad of practical interventions and political campaigns. Self-help fed into Victorian individualism, most famously in John Stuart Mill's *On Liberty* (1859), with its gospel of freedom, diversity, and self-fulfilment in the face of the forces of conformity.

The final instalment of Smiles's series was *Duty; with illustrations of Courage, Patience and Endurance* (1880), a title which reflected the Victorians' prioritization of obligations over rights, and the importance of what Gladstone invoked as 'the rule of Ought' as an imperative which far transcended religious morality. George Eliot famously dismissed God and life everlasting but found the demands of duty 'peremptory and absolute'. The service motive rivalled the profit motive, so much so that one of the most intractable difficulties in the way of acceptance of Darwinian notions of the survival of the fittest was the widespread belief in the overriding instinct to altruism. Duty underpinned imperial effort abroad and philanthropy at home: the *noblesse oblige* of the colonial administrator, and the moral obligation of charitable effort for both men and women.

Frames of mind

Although not strictly components of Victorianism, it would be possible to extend this discussion almost ad infinitum by offering up a longer list of supposedly characteristic Victorian attitudes. A number of classic studies of the Victorians have attempted this, most notably Walter Houghton's *The Victorian Frame of Mind* (1957). Some of Houghton's catalogue, including hero worship, rigidity, and dogmatism, will be taken up in other chapters. Here we can consider a number of attitudes which more commonly feed into hostile definitions of Victorianism, namely materialism, complacency, emotional repression, and racism.

The Victorians were acutely aware of their place in the wider flow of history. Previous cyclical conceptions gave way to progress as the animating principle of historical narratives. Victorian theology, philosophy, anthropology, and sociology were all predicated on assumptions of improvement, although progress was as much desire as description: it did not just happen, it needed to be pursued. 'We are on the side of progress,' Macaulay asserted in 1835. Even where contemporary realities failed to live up to expectations, the Victorians were inclined, in the words of the title of a popular song from music hall and drawing room, to look to the 'Good Time Coming'. From Tennyson's *Locksley Hall* to the novels of George Eliot we can see a confidence in social advancement, however tortuous and complicated it might be in practice.

The Victorians did not just celebrate progress, they invested it with almost religious significance, as another of those criteria by which the world could be divided into the blessed and the benighted, with themselves, naturally, on the side of the angels. Glorying in their visible economic hegemony and imperial superiority, they left themselves vulnerable to the charge that self-confidence was allowed to degenerate into self-satisfaction, smugness, and a selectivity of vision. In 1858, the elite London dining group 'the Club' affirmed that the London of the day represented the highest level civilization had hitherto achieved.

The belief that material and moral progress went hand in hand opened the door to complacency. Not a blindness to problems and challenges, but a focus on what Walter Bagehot described as removable evils, a timidity of approach and a satisfaction with marginal advances which looked dangerously like indifference. The Victorians luxuriated in the manifestations of their remarkable industrial development. The 1851 Great Exhibition and the exhibitionary culture which followed seemed to celebrate artefact and invention almost irrespective of utility or beauty. The homes of all classes became sites of collection and display, the Victorian drawing room or parlour a cluttered capsule of 19th-century commodity culture, and a projection of what the artist Charles Eastlake described as the Victorians' 'lust for profusion'.

Ornamental over-elaboration registered the emphasis on quantity over quality, just as the priority of verisimilitude subordinated affect to accuracy. Truth became beauty. From the beginning of the reign vulgarity and ugliness were the Victorians' self-criticisms of choice. In his *How I Became a Socialist* (1894), the designer William Morris presented his motivation as 'hatred of modern civilisation...its mastery of and its waste of mechanical power...Its eyeless vulgarity...[its] sordid, aimless, ugly confusion'; for the historian E. P. Thompson Morris's memoir represents 'one of the profoundest challenges to "Victorianism" ever written'. Aesthetics are of course a matter of personal preference. But even advocates for the Victorians tend to pause when they reach the question of whether Victorian society was ugly, and concede the weakness of the visual arts.

Perversions of both property and progress shaped the universal but far from uniform racism of Victorian culture. We cannot ignore the strident insistence on ownership rights in people which accompanied the emancipation of slaves in the British empire in the 1830s and 1840s, nor the ways belief in the common humanity of all races was increasingly submerged beneath mutual hostility and the belief in separate development. Nonetheless, this was a racism with limits. Opinion was overwhelmingly hostile to slavery and committed to the development of all races, albeit in a particular westernized version. But even for the most favourably inclined Victorians theoretical commitments to equality were increasingly combined with rigidly hierarchical views which condemned non-western cultures as savage or barbaric and denigrated the intellectual capacities and potential of non-white peoples. From the 1850s onwards discourses of unbridgeable racial difference were widely employed. Blackness, in particular, became a matter not just of display, but of caricature. The English stage came to be dominated by a sort of black grotesque, as in the common 'nigger minstrel' shows, in which Africans or Afro-Americans were portrayed as comic, dependent, and submissive. The willingness of many of the British intellectual elite to rally to the defence of the brutal repression of the uprising in Haiti in 1865, and the casual dismissal of the loss of life caused by colonial wars, even before the emergence of more 'scientific' registers of racism in the 1880s and 1890s, reveal how widespread these tendencies were.

Limits

For all that Victorian Britain was a highly normative society, it was not a highly disciplined one. Ideals were powerful but there was plenty of wriggle room within and space without. A pervasive presence in Victorian evangelicalism was the fear of 'backsliding', of not living up to the ideal, and especially the anxiety that public virtue might coexist with private misbehaviour; the Victorians were perfectly aware of the lurking danger of hypocrisy, the self-conscious inconsistency between public professions and private conduct. Robert Louis Stevenson's *The Strange Case of Dr Jekyll and Mr Hyde* (1886) can in this sense be seen as an allegory of Victorian society more broadly: beneath the civilized Jekyll lurks the bestial Hyde.

Throughout the period empire functioned as a place where at least some of the conventions of Victorian propriety could be temporarily set aside, while at home the clubs and societies of

'Bohemia' offered some relief from many strait-laced restrictions. Wealth also brought its own freedoms. At times it seems that the more eminent the Victorian, the more unorthodox their lives.

Even the most cursory of delves into the private lives of the Victorians throws up these sorts of disparity. Richard Monckton Milnes, MP and man of letters, was also a collector of pornography on a gigantic scale. Dickens abandoned his wife for a young actress. Wilkie Collins and the artist W. P. Frith both maintained two families a few streets apart. The barrister and Working Men's College teacher Arthur Munby and his wife Hannah Culliwick were secretly married for nearly 40 years, throughout which she continued to live as his maidservant while they indulged in elaborate erotically charged role-playing. This sort of eccentricity was as much a part of the Victorian pattern as staid conformity.

It was not just that some Victorians were respectable and some not, but that the line between respectability and its opposites, unrespectability and 'roughness', rarely distinguished different groups of people. Instead, as the historian Peter Bailey has demonstrated, it discriminated between different sorts of behaviour, although this did not stop the boundaries between them being policed even more insistently than those between classes. The fear of moral contagion and pollution remained visceral. The outrage prompted by the music halls of the 1890s focused on their facilitation of undesirable traffic between respectable and unrespectable.

Each Victorian convention was animated by its opposite. Thrift was designed to combat profligacy. Temperance wrestled with drunkenness. Piety was always in uneasy compromise with irreverence. The ubiquity of machinery helps to explain the Victorian preoccupation with fairies. The frequent equation of sentimentality with feminine weakness needs to be balanced by the tears that widely greeted the death of Dickens's Little Nell. The importance of being earnest was confronted by *The Importance of Being Earnest*, whose comedy, like much of Wilde's wit, relied largely on the main characters' subversions of conventional expectations, and willingness to live double lives. It is a measure of the power of these conventions and ideals that while satirizing Wilde was able simultaneously to also reinforce them.

Conventional virtues were not without their counter-intuitive implications: conspicuous consumption could be a form of thrift, storing up domestic assets for pawning in times of financial difficulty. Radical activism was itself often shaped by the conventions it sought to confront. Challenge in one direction was often associated with conventionality in others: often the leaders of the Victorian women's movement, like Josephine Butler, had very conventional views about morality. Greater freedom was often achieved by subverting conventions from within. So women carved out space in the public sphere through the performance of gender stereotypes.

Indeed the operation of Victorian patriarchy offers a telling example of the power of convention but also of its limits, both cultural and chronological. The individual experience of family life was of course almost infinitely varied and generally impossible to ascertain. Although companionate and collaborative marriage was increasingly the ideal, the reality was often more transactional and not infrequently brutal. Separate spheres ideology was entrenched in practice. Marriage institutionalized the subjection of women to men. Married women were frequently barred from paid employment, ceased legally to be able to acquire their own property, and were denied equal access to divorce even in the limited circumstances in which it became possible after 1857, and routinely cut off from all access to their children where separation or divorce occurred. The leading public schools, universities, London clubs, and learned societies were all 'homosocial' institutions which vigorously excluded women. The professionalization of employment, the organization of sport, and even the new definitions of enfranchisement all involved highly effective exclusionary processes of asserting male privilege.

But the wider public sphere was less easily controlled. Women created roles for themselves in female 'auxiliaries' to male societies. They claimed a specific responsibility for religious and philanthropic activities where it could be said that 'feminine' qualities were most needed. By the 1860s and 1870s they were establishing parallel public schools and university institutions, and pioneers like Elizabeth Blackwell and Sophia Jex-Blake were forcing themselves into the medical profession. In the final decades of the period progressive political associations were creating new opportunities for a Beatrice Webb or Margaret Llewellyn Davies.

Nonetheless, barriers remained formidable and exceptions few. Conventional expectations generally denied girls the same educational opportunities as boys. Even when women prised open spaces at Oxford and Cambridge in the 1870s and 1880s they could study but not graduate until after 1901. The contributions of Harriet Taylor to the writings of John Stuart Mill, or Mary Anning's significance in Victorian palaeontology went unacknowledged. Almost all campaigns for greater political rights and access were met with vitriolic misogyny (including from many of the most prominent of Victorian women, not least Queen Victoria herself).

Conclusion

We cannot simply dismiss the idea of 'Victorianism'. It was too much a part of the ways in which observers, and even the Victorians themselves, have tried to make sense of period. And its conventional components can give real insight into the ideas and values by which the Victorians sought to live, or at least felt they ought to live, and so to the sorts of pressures, moral and legal, under which they existed. But we must not make the mistake of treating Victorianism as descriptive. We cannot comprehend the Victorians by their conventions, which offered aspiration as much as actuality. And above all, the uniformity of attitudes and beliefs, never mind behaviour, which 'Victorianism' suggests, was entirely illusory. The Victorians and the world they lived in, were much more varied, more complicated, and more interesting than that.

Chapter 5
Victorian configurations

If we want to understand the particular character of the period, rather than resorting to the ideological characterizations of 'Victorianism' it makes much more sense to look at the contexts and environments in which the Victorians lived and the common experiences they shared. Individual responses were diverse, but the world to which they were responding was shared. The purpose of this chapter is to tease out what was characteristic and distinctive about the Victorian period. To use a musical metaphor, if a previous chapter looked at the movements and the melody, this chapter examines the instrumentation and the harmonics.

We should be clear from the outset that the distinctiveness of the Victorians was rarely, if ever, a matter of uniqueness. Victorian Britain was not a discrete historical box, cut off from what went before and after. Innovations like the railways had both precursors and afterlives. Even transformed elements such as newspapers carried into the period and took out of it considerable continuities. Nor was distinctiveness a matter of unchangeability, except perhaps in some of the components of a moving whole.

At times we see the particular character of the period in the progressive unfolding or articulation of a technological innovation or a social process or a new understanding. At other times we see it in enduring forms like the ubiquitous three-volume ('triple-decker') novel rather than the books' content; in customs and practices but not necessarily the meanings inscribed in them. At times we see it in persistent lines of debate, perennial questions, and nodes of controversy; or in the parameters of the possible. Above all, we can think of the character of the Victorian period as constructed out of distinctive sets of conjunctions and relationships, out of, for example, not so much the presence of the railway or the steamship, but from their particular interrelationships with the still vital horse and sailing ship.

Politics and the state

Victorian politics, bookended by the Reform Acts of 1832 and 1918 (and their equivalents for Scotland and Ireland), illustrates most of these themes. The system established in 1832 was not democracy; it did not even establish the sovereignty of the electorate. (For many, and perhaps most, Victorians 'democracy' continued to be anathema throughout the period.) The right to vote was, after all, entirely male: despite some very limited concessions of the right of single property-owning women to vote in local elections later in the period, Victorian women could not vote for MPs and they could not serve in Parliament. But as a result of the 1832 Act, the franchise and the parliamentary system it underpinned became amenable to progressive readjustment. Eligibility for the franchise remained a matter of personal fitness as much as systemic exigencies, and debates over the nature and claims of citizenship remained at the heart of politics. The reforms of 1867 and the 1880s grafted new voters onto the existing constitution, but they did not fundamentally alter it. Political legitimacy flowed from the popular vote, and elections generally determined governments, but their primary function remained to select individual MPs. A new sort of constitutional monarchy operated: the Queen exerted personal influence but could no longer manipulate electoral politics in the way her predecessors had.

Politics was a matter of patricians within and pressure groups without. The landed ruling class remained pre-eminent; not least because political power continued to be determined more by the distribution of seats than by the size of the electorate. The forces of deference remained formidable. The middle classes exerted greater influence, but ultimately abdicated executive authority to the aristocratic elites. Although it was not easy to manage Parliament from outside the House of Commons, it remained possible. As prime minister, Lord Salisbury sat in the Lords until his death in 1902, along with nine of the cabinet in his 1895–1900 government.

The restricted franchise reinforced the principle of 'virtual representation', whereby the elected represented electors and non-electors (including women) alike, and this ensured that policy-makers were forced to engage with an ill-defined although much-extended and overt 'public opinion'. For all the insulation of government, and foreign policy in particular, from popular influence, Victorian politics remained the politics of external pressure.

Because ultimately qualification to vote could be contested, battles over registration became a characteristic component of constituency politics, reinforcing the importance of local party organization. Pre-Victorian 'Tory' and 'Whig' alignments had been aristocratic connections more than communities of principle or alignments around policy. After 1832 politics came to be organized around the struggle between two parties with distinct political identities, eventually identified as Conservative and Liberal. Very crudely, Conservatives were Anglican, agricultural, and suspicious of change, while Liberals were Nonconformist, urban, and in search of improvement.

Admittedly party alignments were disrupted for a while by the split of the Conservatives over the Corn Laws in 1846 and of the Liberal Party over Ireland after 1885, and both parties were always rather ill-disciplined and unstable coalitions of different interests and views. And admittedly this remained a politics of allegiance rather than of institution, in which relationships between national party leaders and constituency supporters were at best tenuous. But votes in Parliament resolved increasingly along party lines, as did voter choices in general elections. The cloth of Victorian politics only unravelled with the subsequent shift to the politics of programme, signalled by the move of welfare to the centre of political debate in the later 1890s and the establishment of effective independent Labour representation between 1900 and 1906.

If the franchise remained restricted, fascination with politics did not. No one could be in any doubt that politics *mattered* to the Victorians. That it was not organized on class lines if anything intensified its tribal character, in which press, periodical, and associational life were all organized around political affiliations. The years after 1832 brought a more general acceptance of a politically engaged populace. This was an age of oratory, or perhaps more accurately 'the age of discussion', as Bagehot put it, which embodied its commitment to the 'liberal ideal' and representative rationality in debates, mock parliaments, and public meetings. Huge crowds assembled for political rallies and election hustings. The press's verbatim accounts of parliamentary proceedings, local councils, and a wide range of meetings and addresses sustained public speaking as the pre-eminent mode of communication and exchange, and nourished the characteristic Victorian presumption that thinking, talking, and writing about the world could make a difference. The platform was also integral to the rituals and regulation of Victorian Britain's voluntary associations, which became a significant means of adjusting the relationship between the central state and local action.

Politics raised intense passions even though the scope of the Victorian state remained narrow. (Historians have described the Victorian state as a 'delegating-market' state, by which they emphasize central government's preference for working through market mechanisms and authority devolved to local bodies rather than taking direct action itself.) The abandonment of mercantilism (the view dominant in the long 18th century that national prosperity was rooted in the surplus of exports over imports, which encouraged protectionism and high tariffs) meant that for the first time the public finances relied on direct taxation (and income tax in particular) as a permanent peacetime feature, despite periodic promises that it would be phased out. The scope of government expanded but largely in its oversight and regulation roles. The aim was good administration not grand legislation. Low expectations allowed low tax burdens, and the share of national wealth the state absorbed remained small. Progress was made towards a more professionalized bureaucracy, but it was slow and uneven.

In the meantime, although there was some intensification of central control following the formation of the Local Government Board in 1871, the priority of the British state remained the empowerment of local action but not its requirement, and its preferred mechanisms were permissive legislation by which local bodies were authorized but not ordered to undertake certain responsibilities, and model clauses, which made it easier for local bodies to build their own statutory powers. As a result, it is very easy to overestimate the importance of many of the textbook highlights of Victorian legislation, including the 1866 Sanitary Act or the 1870 Education Act, which created structures under which local initiative could operate, but which did not themselves impose new ways of operating across the nation.

Throughout the period most state action was applied and financed unevenly by local government, municipal corporations, parish vestries, and justices of the peace. This activity in turn was marginal to areas such as health and welfare where responsibility was devolved to charitable and philanthropic organizations. As the *Bradford Observer* remarked in 1868, 'Nothing more vividly marks our civilisation than the multiplication of separate societies and agencies, religious, charitable, political, economical, educational, professional, friendly, recreative and what not.' Victorian hospital services, welfare support for the 'deserving poor', and services such as district nursing were all delivered almost entirely outside both national and local state institutions. The reforms of the 1906–14 Liberal governments finally reconfigured this pattern by shifting from the regulatory to the provisionary state, tilting the balance of central–local expenditure decisively and permanently in favour of the centre, and shifting the burdens of social policy from voluntary associations to the state sector.

Economy and society

Throughout the Victorian period Britain was the most industrially advanced economy in the world. Patterns of growth were very uneven, both chronologically and across different sectors, but overall per capita GDP increased by around 200 per cent while Victoria reigned. Manufacturing's share of British GDP peaked in 1901, at which point the share of agriculture had fallen by two-thirds. Output per head improved by 50 per cent from 1870 to 1901. Even so, it is simplistic to think of Victorian Britain as an industrial economy. Land and loans were as important as looms. Agriculture remained the single largest sector into the 1880s, if not beyond. In London and the south-east services, and especially financial services, banking, stockbroking, and insurance, were by far the most lucrative activity. The share of manufacturing in economic output remained virtually unchanged for the whole of the period. Although industry was export focused (e.g. three-quarters of British cotton production went to overseas markets), the value of imported goods greatly exceeded that of exported manufactures throughout the period, and earnings from services, overseas investments, and shipping were needed to keep Britain's international payments in some sort of balance.

Industry was constrained socially as well as economically. Even during the mid-century decades the fortunes left by the commercial and financial men of the City of London easily surpassed those of the industrial middle class, and rivalled those of the landed classes. It is no longer credible to argue as historians once did that the Victorian middle class 'failed', neglecting investment in manufacturing and instead ploughing profits into landed estates and assimilating into the gentry. But whatever the motivations, wealth generated in the industrial north was often transferred into land and financial assets, a process accelerated by mid-Victorian joint stock legislation which greatly extended the opportunities and safeguards of shareholding. And it was only in the final years of the reign that land lost its primacy as the asset of choice of the wealthiest Victorians.

In the same way, the Victorians' experience of work was much more varied than images of factory hands and mineworkers can encompass. Despite mechanization there was a great deal of unskilled and often casual labour in towns and the countryside. Skilled craft labour not only persisted in many building trades but was extended into varieties of engineering work, and there were also expanding opportunities in clerical and administrative functions (as much as 10 per cent of the working population by 1901). Even where manufacturing dominated it was often (as in the case of shoemaking in Leicester or metalworking in Birmingham) through small-scale workshop production which allowed for considerable autonomy in working practice. But to varying degrees all manual workers experienced the same pressures and trajectories, a shift away from piece work to daily and weekly wages, intensifying pressures of control and pace of working, and a hardening of workplace hierarchies and gender distinctions. Work was progressively separated off from the rest of life as the working day and week were more tightly defined and enforced. Long working hours remained the norm: the eight-hour day was not generally adopted until after the First World War. The creation of more defined periods for leisure and recreation, especially Saturday afternoons, bank holidays, and holiday weeks, encouraged a largely instrumental attitude to work, despite the idealization of labour in some quarters, and despite the investment of many larger companies in the provision of sports clubs, recreational buildings, and works outings.

Class identities were unstable, not least because income and wealth were precarious. The period saw enormous wealth creation, but also extraordinary volatility. Technological change could and did undermine the status and position of occupational groups with frightening speed, as the eclipse and immiseration of the Lancashire handloom weavers in the early Victorian period illustrated. A fragile financial system and a wildly cyclical economy brought periodic slumps often associated with banking crises and bankruptcy. Many Victorians, even wealthy ones, lived only one misfortune away from ruin and destitution. There was a heavy dose of relief in the self-satisfaction of the prosperous. Poverty was endemic, especially at certain points in the life-cycle. Young adults or families with wage-earning children could enjoy comfortable incomes, but working-class parents with infants or the elderly often struggled to make ends meet.

At the macro-level, real incomes were on a rising trend for most of the second half of the century, but this only slowly translated into increased consumption across all classes. Much of this was directed to more spending on leisure, and the progress of the haves was balanced by the straitened circumstances of the have-nots. The lesson of Charles Booth's *Life and Labour of the London Poor* (1889–1902) was that as many as 30 per cent of the working class were living in poverty. The working-class diet remained restricted, with little increase in the consumption of dairy products or fresh meat before the 20th century.

Urbanization was the crucible of these contradictions. Victorian Britain was always a nation of small towns as much as large cities. The significance of the frequently quoted statistic that by 1851 more of the population lived in towns than in the countryside is diminished somewhat by the fact that most settlements over 2,000 inhabitants were included in this count. Many 'urban' Victorians were living in small market towns embedded in agricultural districts, in circumstances largely indistinguishable from the rest of the inhabitants of the countryside. Nevertheless, Britain was urban not just for the significant minority of town and city dwellers, but also for the rest of the Victorians, for whom urban growth and the novel landscape of towns and cities came to symbolize the arrival and the challenges of modern society. Almost all the population growth experienced by Victorian Britain was urban. Existing cities mushroomed. Manchester, the symbol of a new age in the 1840s, grew from around 150,000 inhabitants in 1831 to 650,000 in 1901. Smaller towns grew steadily. New towns emerged from nothing; Middlesbrough, an undeveloped farm before 1829, was home to 100,000 by 1901.

The anonymity of the city brought relative freedom from the intrusive surveillance of pre-industrial society. Of course crowded tenements and terraces created new kinds of intimacy; but they also transformed urban geographies, driving wealthier inhabitants from the centre, creating the new phenomenon of the 'suburbs'. The cramming together of urban dwellers brought polluted air and contaminated water. Unregulated house building left most of the working classes without a bath, and most without even an outside WC until the end of the period. Attempts to clear the worst of the 'slums' barely scratched the surface. But urban living also brought opportunity: not just pubs but music halls and sporting clubs; and for the better-off concerts, galleries, museums, and libraries. For many of the elite the social and geographical segregation that urban growth and suburbanization produced was a source of great anxiety, which explains the enormous efforts to bridge the gaps between the classes, to ensure that social solidarity was sustained by more than just the 'cash nexus'.

The Victorians were generally confident in markets and their abilities to operate with minimal regulation, despite periodic financial crises, company fraud, and exogenous emergencies like the 1860s Cotton Famine (the disruption in the supply of cotton caused by the American Civil War). But they recognized exceptions, including the regulation of railways, commenced by the Railway Regulation Act of 1840, which appointed the first railway inspectors, or the municipal supply of water, gas, and later electricity. The implications of the spread of market relations were not only economic, but also social and cultural. Processes of commercialization converted hierarchical relationships of philanthropy and patronage into egalitarian transactions governed by popularity and demand. Customers and their cash rather than cultural elites and their controls came to determine the shape of swathes of social life. In art the emergence of the art dealer and the reviewer helped to replace the aristocratic patron of 18th-century art with the middle-class buyers and working-class consumers of cheap prints. From fiction to the working men's clubs to the music hall, attempts to impose standards of propriety or sobriety from without were defeated by the spending power of the clientele. Conservative voices like the philosopher H. L. Mansel deprecated the 'commercial atmosphere... redolent of the manufactory and the shop' that by the 1860s floated around sensation literature such as M. E. Braddon's notorious *Lady Audley's Secret* (1862).

Victorian spaces

Framed by transformations in communications in the 1830s and the 1900s, the intersections of culture and geography typical of Victorian Britain were another aspect of the period's distinctiveness. At the start of Victoria's reign, improvements in communication, not just the railways and steamships—Tennyson's 'thoughts that shake mankind'—but paper-making machinery, wood-cut illustrations, and cable telegraphy, reordered British space as well as Britain's place in the world. At the same time, the steam press provided a parallel publishing revolution, creating the national market for the popular monthlies and weeklies characteristic of Victorian periodicals, for example *Punch*, the *Illustrated London News*, and the *News of the World*, just three of the new titles launched in the years after Victoria's accession and which were subsequently a prominent feature of Victorian reading culture.

These transformations were always more than just mechanisms of mobility. Rowland Hill's transformation of the postal service in the years around 1840, not just the reduction in price to a penny, but the convenience of the pre-paid adhesive stamp, and a service offering up to six deliveries a day in the larger cities, broke down regional isolation and extended correspondence networks. Letters proliferated like emails. In the six years of his 1880–6 government Gladstone wrote 1,107 letters to the Queen. Meanwhile, the railways brought new ways of seeing, new modes of intellectual exchange, new forms of social solidarity, not to mention a new breed of celebrity civil engineer and their monuments, including Robert Stephenson and the Menai Straits Bridge, Isambard Kingdom Brunel, and William Fairbairn. The geologist Gideon Mantell grumbled that the railways 'completely metamorphosed the English character', inducing 'eternal hustle' and the hunger for constant change.

These technological changes did not, of course, sweep away the old. The railway was a restricted technology whose impact on the British landscape was a great deal less destructive than that of the automobile would be at the start of the 20th century. Horse alongside train characterized the Victorian land transport regime; at sea, sail coexisted with steam. The railways encouraged the development and closer integration of national organization and enabled political leaders, organizing agents, lecturers, and preachers to reach all parts of the country; but within towns and cities horse-drawn carts and omnibuses remained supreme. The expanding rail networks consolidated industrial regionalism while at the same time intensifying regional specialization, accelerating the shift of population from countryside to town and from smaller centres to larger, reversing the concentration of urban population in London by encouraging the growth of a number of large provincial cities and urban hinterlands.

Not that the metropolis wasn't always an enormous presence. Numerically London grew in relative significance, and by the end of the period contained more people than all of Scotland and Wales combined. As the seat of parliamentary power and the home of national societies in science, art, and the professions, it exerted a unique gravitational pull. Its gentlemen's clubs and literary coteries continued to supply social and intellectual leadership. But its sheer size and diversity and fragmentation into innumerable local boroughs and jurisdictions diffused its sense of identity and dissipated its collective voice.

Outside London, Britain remained a patchwork of distinct regions with strong local allegiances. Many of the period's most significant movements and campaigns originated in the provinces or drew their strength from outside the capital. It was an essentially provincial dissenting conscience that fuelled the temperance movement, whose main national organizations were headquartered in Manchester and Bolton. It was the northern textile districts and then later the midlands manufactures that nourished Victorian campaigns for state education. The cooperative movement, which provided value-for-money goods through principles of mutualism, traced its origins back to Rochdale in the 1840s. The founding members of the Football League were all teams from the industrial north and the midlands, just as the development of local amenities and services including gas and electricity owed more to Joseph Chamberlain's 'municipal socialism' than to metropolitan vision.

The Victorian press registers this dispersal of the capital's influence and also its eventual reversal. Setting aside *The Times*, which had attained the status of a national newspaper of record by the start of the period, the press was geographically decentred. Although provincial demand for London papers remained strong, largely because of their coverage of Parliament and foreign affairs, they mostly ignored the provinces, which sustained their own titles with strong local coverage, especially after the repeal of the newspaper taxes in the 1850s allowed for rapid growth.

Provinciality was also characteristic of the Victorian novel, so that Dickens's London was only one location amongst Elizabeth Gaskell's Manchester, Margaret Oliphant's Carlingford, Anthony Trollope's 'Barsetshire', George Eliot's 'Loamshire', Thomas Hardy's Wessex, and Arnold Bennett's Potteries. But all these novelists were published by London publishers, and although to an extent the Edinburgh houses led by William and Robert Chambers held out—while recognizing from the 1840s that they too needed a London office—publishing manifested both continuing conjunctions of centre and locality, and the steady triumph of metropolis over province. The characteristic elements of Victorian publishing, triple-decker novels, serialization, a myriad of periodicals and magazines, and the pervasive influence of Mudie's commercial circulating library, centralized production in London while mediating consumption through local institutions, libraries, and reading rooms.

Belief and doubt

Institutional religion may have been in numerical decline, relatively speaking, but the most salient feature of Victorian Britain was that it remained intensely religious, both in public and in private. Underestimating this is one of the easiest ways to misunderstand the Victorians. The ideas, the institutions, and the rituals of Victorian religion all look so familiar; but the spiritual investment in them is not. Although it did not keep pace with the growing population, church attendance continued to increase in absolute numbers. There was an enormous boom in church and chapel building. Most of those who did not attend regularly considered themselves Christian and kept religious observance of the rites of passage of baptism, marriage, and funeral.

Victorian culture was indelibly marked by denominational conflict, and it was the working out of a limited but tolerated religious pluralism which was more characteristic of the period than secularization. The changes of the 1830s inspired Anglicanism with a new sense of purpose and engendered in Nonconformity a new assertiveness, establishing the competitive *modus vivendi* that was characteristic of the whole period. The beliefs shared by broad-church Anglicanism and mainstream Dissent—the individualism of salvation, the emphasis on the saving atonement of Christ on the cross, and the general acceptance of the Bible as God's revelation—all helped to underpin a dominant Protestantism. At the same time, the many remaining areas of inequality fed discord and played a key role in shaping Victorian party alignments. Anglicanism and Dissent competed to extend their influence, and they clashed over the best way to support the extension of education. More than this, from the 1830s to at least the 1880s they seemed to offer two quite different tempers. Victorian Anglicanism rested on an occasionally worldly mix of establishment status and capacious theology. By contrast what became known as the 'Nonconformist Conscience' sought to measure and mould all aspects of public life to a set of absolute moral standards, upholding purity, temperance, and thrift against the imagined currents of promiscuity, drunkenness, and gambling.

Religion supplied many of the critical lines of political division, and fuelled much social and cultural activism. The communal life of parish and congregation, Sunday schools, mutual improvement associations, welfare societies, and later sports clubs and 'pleasant Sunday afternoons', was as important in the social and cultural life of the nation as the pub or the beerhouse. The intellectual authority of religious institutions declined, but public opinion continued to be educated by the pulpit and the Sunday magazine, and biblical idiom and religious imagery continued to act as powerful forces of continuity and cohesion. William Holman Hunt's painting *The Light of the World* (Figure 3), a portrayal of a human Christ come to save humanity, was so popular that it was said that reproductions hung in almost every home, and it attracted millions of viewers when it toured Australia and New Zealand in 1906.

Religious faith was under pressure, from scientific challenges to the creation narrative and natural theology, from literary-critical challenges to the status of the Bible as the 'word of God', as well as from institutional challenges to the ability of the churches to provide attractive and accessible worship and a message which resonated with the lives and aspirations of all classes. But it was often theology and liturgy that was rejected rather than Christianity, and if doubt was widespread, faith was pervasive. The shifting of certainties should not be mistaken for the triumph of scepticism. The will to believe was strong, and the desire for ethical codes felt urgently. In the words of the Victorian historian Lord Acton, the Victorians were caught 'between the intense need of believing and the difficulty of belief'. They were driven by moral imperatives, whether divine or secular, and the enduring appeal of Carlyle and Ruskin, and of influential American thinkers such as Emerson and Walt Whitman, was their ability to supply an alternative personal ethic and duty, of self-realization and altruism.

Loss of Christian faith was frequently traumatic and for many it was followed by a desperate search for alternatives, as the popularity of spiritualism and 'psychical research' into the 'spirit world' demonstrated. New secular religions, including Owenism and Positivism in the 1840s and Theosophy and the Ethical Societies of the 1880s and 1890s, offered most of the trappings of

3. Holman Hunt, *The Light of the World* (1853).

religious observance shorn of belief in a personal God. While a small minority of 'secularists' and 'freethinkers' waged war on the ideas and institutions of Christianity, most agnostics, like the biologist T. H. Huxley (who coined the word), happily supported the teaching of the Bible in state schools.

Morality did not so much seep into Victorian culture as steep it. Hence the almost universal commitment to learning and teaching, to the instructive quality and the ethical character of all aspects of society and culture, including literature, art, and music. The novelist, Trollope remarked, 'must teach whether he wish to teach or no'. History appealed because it could be treated as a moral storehouse. The populist sensation fiction of the 1860s with its often lurid plots was justified by its exposure of social problems, and even the pornographic *My Secret Life* was defended by its author on didactic grounds. The pre-Victorian penal law and its custodial institutions were remoulded to give priority to what was described as 'the task of inculcating moral character'. Taste in art veered towards genre paintings in which the message was more important than the medium.

It is easy as the period progressed to find younger voices, including the art critic and historian Walter Pater or his student Oscar Wilde, railing against the dead hand of didacticism, calling for an art or a music which privileged beauty and the evanescent response of the emotions. But such aestheticism was always treated with suspicion by the majority. Hedonism was best kept hidden, and Victorian leisure never really escaped from the imperatives of 'rational recreation', the evangelically inspired need to 'improve the hour', to devote 'spare' time to learning, self-improvement, moral reflection, and service to others, to avoid temptations of the flesh.

The Victorians preferred to think about 'recreation' as a complement to work aimed at self-improvement, rather than 'leisure', an idea too readily associated with licentiousness. But we must be careful not to be misled by their anxieties or the institutional preoccupations of contemporaries into making leisure too worthy. It is true that the remnants of early modern cruel sports, dog and cock fighting, were suppressed. Working-class gambling was largely prohibited although not prevented. A great deal of money and effort was invested by churches and municipal authorities in providing improving facilities—parks, libraries, baths, and playing fields—and at times it seemed like similar energies were applied to policing the streets and protecting the Sabbath.

Yet leisure always transcended efforts to tame it. Education never eradicated indulgence. The Victorians had the benefit, in the words of *The Times*, of a 'mingled mass of perfectly legitimate pleasures', of which drinking, gambling, searching out the sensational, the spectacular, and at times the sordid were very much a part. Despite the frequent longueurs of the strict Sunday, looking back Victorians generally recalled non-work lives filled with a great deal of fun, of innocent amusements and pastimes, games, hobbies, shows, and excursions. Muscular Christianity promoted participation in sports and the amateur ideal, but could only delay the emergence of professional spectator sport. The market did not reject rational recreation, as much as rework its elements. Organized religion and politics bowed to the need to be attractive; lectures evolved into comic readings and 'talks', gymnasia gave way to team sports, mutual improvement classes metamorphosed into parliamentary debating societies, without ever abandoning the aspiration to improvement.

The one culture?

This rational imperative helped to give Victorian culture a holistic quality which only dissolved in the face of the increasing specialization of knowledge at the very end of the century. The public prominence of a philosopher like T. H. Green, or a psychologist like Henry Maudsley, reflects the reach of what commentators have described as the Victorian 'common culture' of generalist discussion, which only slowly gave way to narrower disciplinary communities circulating their ideas in specialist journals. There is of course always a danger of concluding too much from the reading and writing of a tiny intellectual elite; but we should not underestimate the extent to which the shared context provided by newspapers, lectures, libraries, and reading rooms disseminated ideas broadly through society.

The Victorians not only thought historically, they were obsessed with time; so much so that they almost invested it, like Lewis Carroll's Mad Hatter, with a personality. Texts like Charles Lyell's *Principles of Geology* (1830–3) forced the Victorians to confront the dramatic extension of the natural time which recent discoveries in geology and palaeontology demanded. They lived for the first time in a world recognizably shaped by change taking place over immense ages. No wonder that when combined with contemporary evidence of rapid technological and economic advance this encouraged a progressivist frame of mind, and a mode of understanding which emphasized the importance of not just seeing a thing as it was, but of recognizing its trajectory—the history of its development, and its potential for the future. One sign of this was the investment of Victorian fiction—with its complex plotting and copious character—in the arts of narration, or the popularity of dramatic monologue and the epic as poetic forms. The novels of Margaret Oliphant or Anthony Trollope in their serial amplitude were an expression of the gradualism, depth, and evolutionary sensibility which resulted.

The irony of the impetus to evolutionary modes of thinking was the way in which this helped sustain an ambivalence towards science. At one level the Victorians embraced science. As innovation by rule of thumb gave way to experimentation and theory, the role of science and men (and only men) of science was acknowledged and celebrated. Provincial scientific and philosophical societies proliferated. Working-class autodidacts and middle-class enthusiasts created vibrant cultures of local amateur botany or entomology. Scientific showmen and flashy experiments became a staple of rational recreation. But 'Stinks', as science was often dismissively called, struggled to escape its second-class status behind the gentlemanly study of Classics. In the public schools and universities it always played second fiddle to the broader arts curricula. Even the provincial mechanics' institutes gradually abandoned hard science for a more miscellaneous mix of subjects. The fierce debates over evolution, which began not with Darwin but in the 1830s and 1840s in response to earlier evolutionary texts, and especially the anonymously published *Vestiges of the Natural History of Creation* (1844), focused as much on the history of evolutionary thought and its implications as they did on the technical biology involved. Literary culture reflected these biases. Sages like Matthew Arnold feared an 'absurdly disproportioned' 'faith in machinery', and for every Ruskin, wrestling with the implications of scientific discovery, there was a William Morris, maintaining a distant distaste.

Science was still transformative. Take the technologies of seeing and showing, and the particular 'culture of looking' that they helped to create. The railway, itself a mode of seeing as well as transport, plate glass windows and glass houses and better and cheaper microscopes, photography, and electrotyping, all shaped a culture quite different from that which had gone before. They encouraged new techniques and extended ways of seeing, royal commissions, statistical investigations, and the urban flâneur, and new ways of showing, including art engraving, the exhibition, and the museum. Coexisting with the fickle and flickering illumination of gaslight and candle, these prompted a culture suspended in tension between what one theorist has called the 'frenzy of the visible', and new anxieties about the possibility of ever seeing accurately.

Inspired by the theories of the French philosopher Michel Foucault, historians have identified a wide-ranging set of institutions of social surveillance, not just those already mentioned, but the new police forces, district visitors, municipal inspectors, and an intensification of record-keeping forms of bureaucracy, the manager's logbook, the timesheet, the personnel file. It is doubtful that these secured the sort of 'panoptic' visibility occasionally ascribed to them, but they certainly contributed to the Victorians' sense of living under an unprecedented degree of scrutiny.

Victorian visuality was marked by a transformation of the production and circulation of images and a heightened interest in 'illustration'. We can see this in the novel relationships of text and image provided by illustrated fiction, rooted in a powerful interpenetration of word and image. As exemplified by the illustrated periodicals, most prominently the *Illustrated London News* (1842), but also the *Art Journal* (1839), and the *Builder* (1843), this was a visuality that was monochromatic and linear, intimate rather than panoramic. We can also see it in the pull of ideals of fidelity and authenticity which pervaded the art of the Pre-Raphaelites and the theatrical productions of actor/managers like Charles Kean. Although it is an overused term, we see it in the overwhelming investment in 'realism' of Victorian fiction, the researched settings of social novels from Gaskell to Gissing, the complex engagements with contemporary ideas and conditions in the novels of Eliot or Henry James, fastidious even in their fantasies. We can see it in the delight in mimesis, and the representational imperatives of Victorian design, the artificial flowers, the porcelain animals, the foliage of Morris wallpaper. Even if, as John Ruskin argued in his *Modern Painters* (1843–60), right seeing did not come naturally, but required careful training, the emphasis in Victorian culture remained on the power of observation. This is not to deny an interest in things not seen or heard, in what George Eliot memorably described as the roar that lies on the other side of silence. But plot not psychology, or mental states and intellectual character which could be located in particular organs of the brain, was the Victorian preference.

Steam engines apart, there was perhaps little that was truly distinctive in the Victorian soundscape. But urban growth and industrial development did bring an intensification of noise: factory engines, clogs and cartwheels on cobbles, the cries of newspaper boys, organ-grinders. More sensitive Victorians, and Carlyle was famously one of these, were at times driven to distraction and the considerable expense of soundproofing by street noises. It was said that in 1869 the dying Lord Amberley was frightened by noise in the street into thinking that revolution had broken out. We should probably take such accounts with a pinch of salt. Sensitive types talked about the tyranny of noise, but Victorian men in particular had plenty of respites: the study, the reading room, the club.

And we need to balance these neuroses with a recognition of the easily overlooked extent to which much of Victorian life deliberately eschewed silence for the pleasures of talk. The Victorians talked in pubs and clubs, on street corners, and in railway carriages, and discussed papers in learned societies and debating clubs. To be a lively talker was more crucial to success in Victorian Britain than to be an effective writer. The working classes did not perhaps share the incessant rounds of conversation at breakfasts, lunches, 'at homes', dinners, and 'soirées', but their homes were similarly the site of collective reading, discussions with friends and neighbours, and gossip. And this sort of domestic talk was not subject to the same exclusionary boundaries as other intellectual exchange, so it drew in mothers, wives, and daughters, society conveners like Lady Victoria Welby, hostesses of literary salons like Anna Maria Hall or Jane Loudon, and labour activists in the making like Margaret Macmillan.

If Victorian society had a sensory pathology it was of smell, both odour and the act of smelling. Although the human capacity to become inured to smells sometimes produces a patchy historical record, there can be little doubt that Victorian Britain was pungent. Personal hygiene could leave a lot to be desired, even making allowances for the limited access to running water and washing facilities. Tennyson was notoriously careless, and frequently needed reminding to wear clean clothes. Rudimentary sanitation and industrial pollution also meant that watercourses were often little better than open sewers: the 'Great Thames Stink' of the long hot summer of 1858 even forced the abandonment of sittings in Parliament.

It was not merely a question of fetid cellars and malodorous sculleries. Urban and rural environments reflected the more general challenge of preservation and disposal, smelling, as one account put it, of 'stale fruit and vegetables, rotten eggs, foul tobacco, spilt beer, rank cart-grease, dried soot, smoke, triturated road dust and damp straw', and this litany ignored the still pervasive smell of horse dung and for many towns the overlying odours of mechanization, the 'stifling smell of hot oil' which Dickens described in 'Coketown'. There was an element of social othering at work here, and a reflection of the Victorian acceptance of 'miasma' theories—the belief that foul smells were carriers of disease—that was only dispelled at the end of the century as germ theory gained acceptance.

Conclusions

The Victorian period was a time of extraordinary dynamism, and nothing in this chapter should be read as denying the extent to which it saw the transformation of Britain. Looking back from 1897 or 1901, what struck Victorians was not stability but change, the distance travelled and the improvements made from 1837. They revelled in the miles of railways constructed, the numbers of newspapers being read, the growth of towns. Yet in doing so they celebrated a narrative of absorption and evolution, the absence of fundamental disruptions or upheavals, the continuities of monarchy, national identities and imperial power, the augmentation of aspects already established early in the reign. By 1901 it was clear that a fresh wave of technological and institutional innovations, the internal combustion engine, cinema and radio and other applications of electricity, welfare policies and Labour politics, were going to bring fresh and fundamental changes, but their effects were as yet minimal. The changes the Victorians experienced had extended, intensified, and augmented, but in most respects had left the underlying forms and overarching structures remarkably untroubled.

Chapter 6
Eminent and less eminent Victorians

So who were the Victorians?

Not everyone who lived in the Victorian period is usefully described as a 'Victorian'. Take someone like Charlie Chaplin, even though he was already 12 when Victoria died. Helping to comprise the populations born, raised, and sent to school in the last years of the reign didn't make Chaplin and his contemporaries Victorian. They were essentially 20th-century figures. Those younger than Chaplin would have scarcely had personal memories of the period. We might say something similar of those who were already in later life when Victoria became queen, even if they lived on well into the Victorian period. Figures like Lord Melbourne, Victoria's first prime minister, or the astronomer and woman of science Mary Somerville, who lived to 1872, represented a pre-Victorian sensibility. That still leaves at least everyone born perhaps from the later 1780s, the oldest of whom would have lived their formative years before 1837 but who were still shaped by and helped to shape the period, including figures such as Thomas Carlyle (1795–1881), and anyone whose adolescence and education were Victorian, certainly anyone born before the early 1880s, which includes, as we have seen, some of the most significant figures of the 20th century.

To get a sense of who these Victorians were, we need to operate at the level both of the population and of the individual. Both perspectives have Victorian resonances. The Victorians and their continental contemporaries were the first to develop an understanding of the statistical principle of the 'population', of normal distributions; they collected and interrogated social data in the aggregate. At the same time, they followed Carlyle in believing that history was 'the essence of innumerable biographies', and Smiles in thinking that right conduct was best inculcated through exemplary lives.

If the Romantics invented celebrity, the Victorians raised it to new heights. They celebrated public figures in prints, cartoons, and pottery figurines, and enthusiastically embraced the pen portrait and ultimately the magazine interview. Although there was no monument to national heroes, commemoration in Westminster Abbey partly served this purpose, and Britain's greatness was manifested through the National Portrait Gallery (established 1856) and the monumental *Dictionary of National Biography*. Victoria's jubilees in 1887 and 1897 were celebrated with tableaux of the reign's heroes. In becoming acquainted with them we are getting to know the Victorians as they sought to know themselves.

Of course selecting 'eminent Victorians' is not without its pitfalls. There are canonical Victorians—real and fictional—just as there is canonical Victorian literature. Even a cursory examination of histories of the period reveals the same characters and characteristics recurring: an unamused Victoria, bickering Gladstone and Disraeli, Ruskin and Carlyle, the misogynistic cultural critics, patient Darwin 'discovering' evolution, intrepid Livingstone and Stanley meeting in some African clearing, Florence Nightingale the nursing 'battleaxe', professionally outrageous Wilde; not to mention neglected Oliver Twist and ingenious Sherlock Holmes. And just as canonical literature can be stereotyped and only partially representative, so confining attention to canonical individuals risks offering a limited and unrepresentative stock cast. After all, eminence is by definition a function of exceptionality, if not idiosyncrasy.

A fully representative picture of the Victorians needs to go further, and include the prosaically popular and the boringly conventional as well as the exceptional. So alongside Tennyson and Swinburne there must be space for the poet of bourgeois 'proverbial philosophy', Martin Tupper. Alongside Thackeray and Trollope, room for Rhoda Broughton, and other 'queens of the circulating libraries' whose conventional fiction was read in vast quantities. With Darwin and Huxley needs to be placed the Christian evolutionist Benjamin Kidd, whose *Social Evolution* (1894) was the largest selling non-fiction title in late Victorian Britain. And beyond this we need to think about the approximately 70 million individuals who lived in the period long enough to qualify as 'Victorians', listed in the census, and massed together in the parliamentary blue books, and understand the arithmetic of the Victorians as a whole, their shared characteristics, the coteries and collectivities—the mass movements, as well as the personalities, the mundane as well as the exceptional.

Victorian demography

After all, Victorian Britain was crowded. We see plenitude and proliferation in W. E. Frith's painting of *Derby Day* (1856–8), in the densely populated novels of Dickens, in the cumulated instances of the statistical movement. This recognition was hardly surprising. The population of Britain (excluding Ireland) soared between the middle of the 18th century and 1914. In 1831, 23.9 million people lived in the British Isles. By the end of the reign this had increased to 41.5 million. This is still of course a long way from the *c.*65 million that the United Kingdom manages to accommodate in the 2020s. But the 19th-century population was not just growing fast, it was relocating internally, constantly outstripping the provision—houses, churches, and schools—available to it. From its establishment in 1837 the General Register Office provided a tabulated summary of what was all too apparent in overcrowded slums, large families, and an often overstocked labour market. Fertility levels were high. The burdens of childbearing did encourage a degree of abstinence, but access to contraception was almost non-existent and 10 or even 12 children to a family was not uncommon.

Sickness was widespread. Debilitating illness was a common burden, and the performance of hypochondria often elaborate. The poorer classes were frequently malnourished, flea-ridden, and lice-infested. Tuberculosis ('consumption'), typhus, measles, and diphtheria were endemic, their danger compounded by periodic epidemics of cholera, scarlet fever, and smallpox. Even in the 1900s it was estimated that half of all working-class women suffered permanent ill-health. Restricted diets and sickness stunted growth: between 1845 and 1904 the normal minimum height for army recruits fell from 5´6″ to 5´. Victoria herself was only 4´10″, though in her case not from want of nourishment, and at times it seems that the health of the more prosperous classes was no better than that of the poor. The philosopher Herbert Spencer was so frequently bedridden that he had forms printed for declining invitations because of ill-health. Grant Allen and Aubrey Beardsley were just two of the prominent Victorians who suffered from tuberculosis. Health spas offering hydrotherapy, rest, and recuperation multiplied. The Victorians, and Victorian intellectuals in particular, seem to have been especially vulnerable to mental breakdown. Ruskin, Pugin, Florence Nightingale, and the painter Edwin Landseer are just a handful of many who suffered persistent mental ill-health.

But if the Victorians often paraded their morbidities, they generally passed over their disabilities, and made little allowance for the obstacles disability created. The Manchester educational reformer John Watts lived his whole life with a marked limp as a result of childhood scarlet fever, but it would be virtually impossible to know this from the public record of his extensive activities. While the abundance of disabled characters in Victorian fiction suggests a reservoir of sympathy, a range of conditions including blindness, deafness, and dumbness, but also epilepsy and even left-handedness, were readily treated as signs of mental handicap. Education for blind and deaf children improved markedly, but opportunities remained highly restricted for all but the most fortunate. Deafness brought exclusion from conversational cultures, and only a tiny number of deaf Victorians were able to carve out a public career. Perhaps the most prominent was Harriet Martineau, who became deaf at 18 and took up writing as the only occupation fully open to her; another was Arthur James Wilson, a cyclist and journalist credited with being the originator of cycle road clubs, who adopted the first name Faed, an anagram of deaf, which he became after contracting scarlet fever. Despite the work of campaigners such as Elizabeth Gilbert, founder of the Association for the Promoting of the General Welfare of the Blind, and occasional examples, of whom the economist Henry Fawcett was perhaps the most prominent, blindness remained an even more effective bar to success.

Part of the problem was the limits of medical science and provision. Lack of preventative knowledge (germs were only identified in the 1880s) and effective treatment meant that disease tied all social groups together. Although medicine advanced, misdiagnosis was common, treatments were often little more than ineffectual attempts to mitigate symptoms, and before the development of antiseptic medicine and anaesthetics pioneered by Joseph Lister and Sir James Simpson hospitals were hardly healthy places. As a result, with sickness came the inescapable presence of premature death. Infant mortality was horrifically high throughout the period, falling only slowly in the 1880s and 1890s, before declining rapidly after 1902. The experience of bereavement was an almost universal part of Victorian parenthood, sometimes on a traumatic scale. In 1856, A. C. Tait, future Archbishop of Canterbury, and his wife Catherine lost five of their six daughters (aged from 18 months to 10 years old) to scarlet fever in the space of eight weeks. Even for the fortunate ones who lived through infancy, life expectancy—a measure of the rate of mortality rather than a prediction of a 'normal' life span—was low even if it was rising.

Hardly surprising, then, that the Victorians elevated dying into an art and mourning into an industry. They were intimate with death, and with the enduring legacy of grief. Organized religion continued to leverage the fear of damnation and the importance of a good death, but the paraphernalia of mourning, the funerary teapots and notepaper, the black dress and jet jewellery, the elaborate coffin furnishings and ornate tombs, were shared by religious and unreligious, rich and poor, alike. In the context of the Queen's notorious 20-year obsequies, or the excesses of the Duke of Wellington's 1852 state funeral with its overloaded carriage coffin too heavy for the 12 horses attempting to pull it, it is tempting to dismiss these practices as signs of an unhealthy fixation with death or a vulgar preoccupation with status. But we should not underestimate the fear of a pauper's grave, nor the extent to which Victorian rituals of death were coping mechanisms, a way of denying the rupture of death through anticipation of the afterlife, and the celebration of lives well lived.

Social structure: class

Of course, if the Victorians were united in sharing the consequences of human frailty, disease, and death, they were divided by various structures which influenced their social position, their identity, and ultimately their life chances. Although class no longer has the hegemonic hold it once had on the way we think about Victorian society, and was at best only one of these structures, it remains the obvious place to start. Divisions within classes were often policed as fiercely as differences between them, but we can say that the Victorians lived for the first time in a society where class identities, manifest in clothes, in access to railway carriages, in consumption and conversation, trumped all others. Individual social mobility was possible, and indeed downwards it was alarmingly easy, but collectively the barriers were formidable. It was possible to acquire status through education or money, and as a result, intergenerational mobility was far greater than the Victorians themselves recognized. But antecedents counted, and class was as much a matter of breeding as of wealth.

Victorian Britain was an aristocratic society. The aristocracy and gentry continued to dominate politics, the diplomatic and armed services, the Church, and the law. After attendance at the handful of leading public schools, followed by Oxford or Cambridge (where high living and hunting preceded an ordinary degree), or via the various military and Indian service colleges, aristocratic sons proceeded naturally into constituencies controlled by family interests and influence, public service, and political office. Gladstone and Disraeli were the only two of Victoria's prime ministers who were not aristocrats, and Disraeli acquired a country house and then title two years into his second premiership. The landed classes provided the membership of the London clubs, maintained the salons at which the business of politics was conducted, and later hosted the country house weekends where the elite shot and cemented their sense of *noblesse oblige*. Unlike in many parts of the Continent this was not a closed caste, and alongside it a combination of intermarriage and powerful dynasties of prominent thinkers, including the Stracheys, the Russells, and the Macaulays, created what has been described as an 'intellectual aristocracy' which transcended the strictly economic boundaries between landed and middle classes.

For all this, the aristocracy did not set the cultural tone. Instead, much of what we understand as archetypically 'Victorian' was characteristically middle class, an identity that was only finally emerging out of what had previously usually been called the 'middling classes' as the reign began. The Victorian middle class was a mixture of professional, industrial, and commercial interests, an enormous diversity tied together by little more than absence of landed wealth and freedom from manual labour, though increasingly also united by education and lifestyle. Most Victorian sages and thinkers came from middle-class backgrounds, following the traditional path to university, and thence to the bar, the Church, journalism, or officialdom. John Stuart Mill was an official of the East India Company, Matthew Arnold was a school inspector. Later in the period H. G. Wells spent his early life as a draper's apprentice and then teacher, reflecting the huge expansion of white collar employment as the reign progressed.

Although the idea of the commercial middle class might initially conjure the factory owner or provincial merchant, its wealthiest and most influential members came from finance: it was the City of London and what historians have described as its 'gentlemanly capitalists', bankers, stock and insurance brokers, and those living off investments, who formed the middle-class elite. The mercantile and industrial middle classes, especially those from the provinces, had a stonier path to eminence: involvement in 'trade', never mind the more demeaning business of making things, continued to carry a social stigma. There was always a place for outsiders like the industrialists Richard Cobden and John Bright, who both moved from pressure group politics to cabinet positions, but it was easier for second and third generations like Sir Robert Peel, Austen Chamberlain, or the essayist William Rathbone Greg to achieve full acceptance.

The timing of the emergence of the working class, and the extent of its cohesiveness remain a matter of debate. E. P. Thompson's foundational text *The Making of the English Working Class* (1963) contended that it formed in the years up to the 1830s. Certainly the language of class was widely adopted at this point, although it coexisted with more populist languages, in which 'the people' or 'ordinary folk' were ranged against rulers or the wealthy. Until later in the century the distinctions of skilled, unionized craft 'labour aristocrats', semi-skilled factory workers, and largely unskilled labourers make it impossible to think of a working class unified in anything other than its reliance on weekly wages. It was only perhaps towards the end of the reign that a more homogeneous working-class culture coalesced around new forms of commercial leisure, spectator sport, and literature aimed at the products of the new Board schools.

Wherever the balance lies, the fate of most of the working classes was anonymity. Setting aside a handful of well-known fictional characters, Alton Locke, Felix Holt, Tess Durbeyfield, the Victorian working classes were largely seen *en masse*, in slum descriptions and statistical accounts, in the occupational typologies of the pioneering sociologist Henry Mayhew, or the crowd scenes of Luke Fildes's *Applicants for Admission to a Casual Ward* (Figure 4). Radicalism provided one environment in which working-class voices like that of the Lancashire weaver-poet Samuel Bamford could distinguish themselves, although the leaders of early Victorian radicalism were rarely themselves working class. From mid-century, trade unionism and the cautious willingness of the Liberal Party to accept working men as parliamentary candidates in the handful of constituencies where the working classes formed a coherent majority of the electorate provided a conduit for a Robert Applegarth, a carpenter who served on a Royal Commission, or a Henry Broadhurst, the stonemason who became the first working-class cabinet minister. Labour history has recuperated the contributions of many others, from the first leaders of the 20th-century Labour Party, Keir Hardie, Ramsay Macdonald, and Arthur Henderson downwards. Otherwise the openness of Victorian society was restricted to the gifted few whose mobility through education or self-improvement involved shedding their working-class identity: figures like the Cambridge scientist William Whewell, son of a carpenter.

4. Luke Fildes, *Applicants for Admission to a Casual Ward* (1874).

Social structure: race

Overlaid on these economic gradations were other distinctions, of gender, religion, and of race, an issue which was never far from the surface of Victorian cultural and intellectual life, but in ways quite different from those pertaining 120 years later.

Not least this is because Victorian Britain was white. Not exclusively, of course. There were no formal controls over immigration, and the legacies of Britain's slave-trading and slave-owning past, and the consequences of the nation's hegemony over global trade, included the residence, both temporary and more permanent, of men and women of colour. There were small numbers of freed slaves, domestic servants who had travelled with families returning from empire, and immigrants. The 'sailortowns' of Britain's ports, where seafarers between ships lived alongside dockers and other casual labourers, were a melting pot of races. Modern efforts to challenge the invisibility of this experience have uncovered a number of personal stories: including Sarah Forbes Bonetta, 'adopted' by Queen Victoria, but largely living in West

Africa as the wife of a Lagos businessman, William Cuffay the Afro-Caribbean Chartist, William Darby the black circus owner, Samuel Coleridge-Taylor, a mixed-race late Victorian composer, and the Bajan immigrant Daniel Tull, whose son Walter became Britain's first professional black football player.

The significance of all of them is their exceptionality: outside London's sailortown we are still talking primarily about individuals and not communities. There are no statistics to fall back on, but data from the work of Thomas Barnardo's charity confirms the 'whiteness' suggested by surviving images of Victorian crowds. The Victorians' encounter with other races came instead through the pages of missionary magazines, imperial adventure tales, or the modest ebb and flow of temporary visitors—students, litigants, transatlantic anti-slavery advocates like Frederick Douglass, actors like Ira Aldridge, or colonial spokesmen like Behramji Malabari. Although her residence was longer and her assimilation to a 'British' identity stronger, something of the same could be said of the Crimean war nurse Mary Seacole, whose *Wonderful Adventures* (1857) made her by far the most prominent 'black Victorian'.

This did not of course make Victorian Britain exclusively Anglo-Saxon. Victorian society reflected the wider legacies of centuries of migration, of French Huguenots, German Jews, American Loyalists, Anglo-Indian nabobs, and Irish navvies. By the end of the period there were as many as 3.5 million Irish-born inhabitants in England, Wales, and Scotland, and perhaps twice that number whose ethnic background was Irish. London continued to be a haven for continental radicals seeking asylum. The Rossetti siblings, Dante Gabriel, founder of the Pre-Raphaelites, Christina, the poet, and William Michael, their memorialist, offer one example amongst many of the processes of migration and absorption which enriched Victorian culture, their father, an aristocratic Catholic Italian forced into exile in the 1820s by his revolutionary nationalism, just as James Whistler, Henry James, and Winston Churchill's mother Jenny remind us of the significance of the American influx later in the century. These presences were not confined to the major population centres: even unexceptional industrial towns like South Shields had small but not insignificant immigrant populations, mostly from northern Europe.

The passing over of the signs—both of facial features and skin tone—which suggested that both Robert Browning and Elizabeth Barrett Browning had mixed-race ancestry, speaks of a culture largely untroubled by anxieties about colour. So long as immigrant populations were small and wealthy, they posed little threat. 'Foreignness' in this sense was no absolute bar to acceptance or success, especially within local communities. Members of the Anglo-Irish 'ascendancy' found few barriers, as the careers of Palmerston, Wilde, Lecky, or Yeats attest. Manchester's Jewish community played a pivotal role in many of the city's cultural institutions, not least the Hallé Orchestra, while the wealth of the Rothschilds provided an entrée to the highest rungs of London society.

This is not to deny the strong undercurrent of casual racism as well as sometimes obstinate legal barriers. While as an Anglican Disraeli could sit in Parliament, it was not until 1858 after 10 years of struggle that Lionel Nathan de Rothschild was permitted to take his seat. But it was the combination of race, religion, poverty, and numbers which was toxic. It was the poor Catholic Irish immigrants of the 1830s and 1840s and impoverished Eastern European Jews of the 1880s and 1890s who elicited overt racism. The prejudice and hostility faced by the Catholic Irish in Britain helps explain why, before the advance of organized labour in the final years of the period brought to national prominence a figure like J. R. Clynes, most prominent Victorian Catholics were middle-class Irish immigrants or English converts.

Sexualities and gender

The minorities that were most systematically and effectively effaced in Victorian culture and its subsequent history were not racial, but sexual, although there are difficulties in applying 21st-century identities to a culture in which even the concept of 'homosexuality' was alien, and in which the homosociality of the public school or Oxbridge college and of female partnerships outside marriage consistently blurred the boundaries of same-sex desire. Male homosexual acts were only formally made illegal after 1885, lesbian acts were never brought under the law; but moral proscription operated powerfully, pushing homosexual cultures underground. The significance of the notorious treatment of Oscar Wilde, whose relationship with Lord Alfred Douglas, and subsequent attempt to sue Douglas's father the Marquess of Queensbury, brought him ostracism, two years' imprisonment with hard labour in Reading Gaol, and a premature death, was that it occurred only at the very end of the period, and was entirely unexpected to many of those involved, including Wilde himself. There are many examples, including Walter Pater and the Cambridge philosopher Henry Sedgwick, of Victorians whose same-sex desires were sublimated or suppressed by cords of self-discipline and peer pressure. And instances like the Eton tutor William Cory who was dismissed for encouraging intimacy (not necessarily sexual) between the boys, or the persecution which drove the artist Simeon Solomon into poverty, are balanced by the more openly acknowledged homosexuality of the cultural historian John Addington Symonds, or the utopian socialist Edward Carpenter.

And we need to set such examples alongside the history of the six children of Edward White Benson, Archbishop of Canterbury from 1883 to 1896, none of whom married or, as far as it is possible to tell, ever had heterosexual sex, and one of whom, his daughter Maggie, lived after Benson's death with her mother, her mother's partner (a daughter of the previous Archbishop), and her own female partner. All of which perhaps reinforces how far for Victorian women the gradations of same-sex partnership were even more complicated: social and economic pressures as well as sexual preference drawing women like the suffragette Louisa Garrett Anderson and her partner Flora Murray, or Frances Power Cobbe and the sculptor Mary Lloyd, into close same-sex relationships, many of which may well have been purely practical and platonic, but many of which were probably more.

As was the case with the rest of the Victorian moral code, responses to unconventional sexualities were powerfully inflected by class. It was quite possible for Lady Ashburton, one of the banking Baring family, to live a complicated life of marriage combined with relationships or affairs with other men and women without sanction or ostracism; whereas Major-General Sir Hector Macdonald, a rare example of a British general who had worked his way up from the ranks, committed suicide in 1903 in the face of an impending court martial over accusations of homosexuality during his command in Ceylon.

Women outnumbered men in Victorian Britain, but conventional lists of eminent Victorians were almost exclusively male, a reminder both of the limits placed on women's activities and the dismissal of their achievements. The society magazine *Vanity Fair* published 1,695 of its famous cartoons of public figures from 1869 to the end of the reign; but the number of women represented did not get into double figures. No wonder eminent women frequently adopted a male persona, as did George Eliot and Vernon Lee, or presented themselves as wife, as did Mrs Gaskell, Mrs Humphry Ward, and innumerable others. The only two Victorian women honoured with burial in Westminster Abbey were the philanthropist Angela Burdett-Coutts and the social reformer Beatrice Webb. In Burdett-Coutt's case the magnificence of her wealth and her extensive philanthropic activities overcame all obstacles.

Otherwise, especially—but by no means exclusively—in fields where they could mobilize Victorian gender roles, and in the various forms of the Victorian women's movement, women did increasingly carve out space not just for activity but for leadership, whether it be the philanthropic work of Octavia Hill, later one of the founders of the National Trust, Maria Rye's emigration campaigns, Julia Margaret Cameron as photographer, even Lady Butler as war artist and Mary Kingsley as explorer. In contrast, only at the end of the century did working-class politics or the suffrage movement offer a route for figures like Margaret Bondfield or Annie Kenney from the humblest of backgrounds.

Life-cycle categories

By the age of 10 Kenney was already working in a Manchester cotton mill. Yet in spite of the persistence of this sort of child labour, the Victorians were especially attentive to and perhaps even especially anxious about childhood—unsurprisingly, given that despite the fragility of young life a third of the population throughout the period were under 15. Urbanization and industrialization heightened concerns about the vulnerability of children. Developments in biology and psychology directed attention to the complexities of the gradual development of infants into adults. Both encouraged the recognition of childhood as a distinct phase of life, requiring legislative protection and educational provision.

But if childhood was newly conceptualized it remained curtailed. For the working classes it ended before teenage years even after the school leaving age was extended; most children would have been working (unpaid if not paid) from the ages of 8 or 9. Wealthier children were often merely driven by different disciplines of education and improvement. The age of sexual consent was only raised from 12 in 1875, and to 16 in 1885. The Edwardian Scouting movement was an implicit acknowledgement of the need to cater for an adolescence only slowly being acknowledged. Victorian children were written up, and written for, but rarely allowed to write themselves, except in dutiful letters and self-surveilling diaries. A Victorian actress like Ellen Terry, already married at 16, might achieve celebrity young, and the juvenilia of the Brontë sisters have become integral to their cultural identity, but generally precocity was frowned upon, and most well-known Victorian children are fictional: Little Nell, Paul Dombey, Oliver Twist, Alice, Peter Pan and Wendy.

Superficial acquaintance with life expectancy figures (which scarcely exceeded 40 by the end of the reign) might suggest a society with few old people. But this was not so (not least because the figures often quoted were depressed by heavy infant mortality). In fact, the common Victorian image of vastly bearded elder statesmen is not entirely misleading. Victorian society was becoming older. Having survived to 18 the average member of the Victorian middle class could reasonably expect to live into their sixties (it was less for manual labourers), and many lived into their seventies and eighties. Ruskin, despite mental illness in later life, lived to 81, Florence Nightingale and the evolutionary biologist and socialist A. R. Wallace to 90. And the availability of pensions only for the fortunate few and little conception of the idea of 'retirement' meant that Victorians also remained active longer, and institutional leadership frequently remained in the hands of the old. Gladstone was prime minister at 83. Tennyson was poet laureate from his early forties to his death in 1892 in his early eighties. The average age of the archbishops of Canterbury was over 75.

One consequence was the quite widespread sense by the 1890s that the natural cycles of ageing and replacement were being clogged up by elderly Victorians lingering on ungraciously. Younger adults were beginning to identify as a post-Victorian *generation*, construing their revolt as against Edwardian uncles and aunts, and Victorian grandparents. In many respects this was a new sort of identity. The Victorians had rarely seen themselves in generational terms. And yet in loose and inconsistent ways they did manifest generational patterns, different perspectives, different tastes and fashions, and it is possible to discern a sequence of generations from early Victorian to Edwardian each of whose greatest influence aligns with the four sub-periods (and subsequent Edwardian period) outlined in Chapter 2. The mid-Victorian establishment including Gladstone and Disraeli were often born between the later 1790s and 1813. Doubters and sages including Arnold, Ruskin, and Huxley were largely a subsequent generation; here we find Victorian anxiety in its fullest flowering, while members of the next generation, including Leslie Stephen and Frederic Harrison, were more assertive in their secularism and confident in their Liberalism. In contrast the late Victorian generation, including Idealists like Patrick Geddes as well as Labour leaders such as Keir Hardie, inclined to a more collectivist interpretation of society, one which by the Edwardian generation had emerged not only in the full-blown socialism of Ramsay Macdonald and H. G. Wells, but also in the more statist Liberalism of L. T. Hobhouse and David Lloyd George.

Celebrities of various sorts

As well as these social collectivities, patterns of celebrity offer a rough index of the status of different aspects of Victorian life. What does the Victorian panorama of pre-eminence reveal? And if we are to construct a broader cast of significant Victorians, who might we include?

If we take our cue from the various celebratory surveys of the reign, pride of place would go to Victorian politicians. Given the attention afforded to political leaders elsewhere in this volume we can perhaps pass over them here, and attend instead to the commentators on politics and public affairs who were given almost equal prominence. The practice of unsigned journalism and an emphasis on the collective voice of the serious periodicals meant that individual voices emerged only slowly across the reign.

Thomas Mozley's thousands of leaders for *The Times* probably made him one of the most influential writers of the period, but he remained unknown to almost all his readers. In the early years it was editors, John Thadeus Delane, editor of *The Times*, 1841–77, or literary editors such as Thackeray, M. E. Braddon, and Dickens himself, who wielded influence. J. G. Lockhart, editor of the *Quarterly Review*, 1826–53, exemplified the tendency of successful early Victorian writers to freelance for many publications and thereby make the transition to a literary career as journalist, critic, and miscellaneous writer. There are innumerable examples of these jobbing journalists and writers, including the essayist G. A. Sala and the adventure novelist G. A. Henty. But this context also produced Walter Bagehot, editor of *The Economist*, whose collections of essays, especially *The English Constitution* (1867) and *Politics and Physics* (1872), provide an unrivalled insight into the workings of Victorian government.

As the period progresses, so Victorian intellectual life was institutionalized in the universities and the newspaper press. Older university scholars, like Benjamin Jowett, continued for a while to exercise an influence across Victorian culture through the depth of their personal connections. They were joined by the sages like Carlyle and Ruskin wielding influence through contributions to the serious periodicals supplemented by networks of correspondence and conversation. From the 1860s it is possible to see a new breed of graduates, like John Morley at the *Pall Mall Gazette* and Leslie Stephen at the *Cornhill*, who saw the 'higher journalism' as a means of finding a political voice. The era of the campaigning editor and the 'press baron' was still largely in the future, although W. T. Stead, who succeeded Morley at the *Pall Mall Gazette* in the 1860s and 1870s, did much to introduce what became known as the 'new journalism', not least its sensational causes, which in the case of Stead's crusade against the exploitation of young girls, 'The Maiden Tribute of Modern Babylon', got him imprisoned. Provincial newspaper editors like C. P. Scott of the *Manchester Guardian* could exercise considerable local influence. At the same time, the conventional forms of pressure group politics, including associational newspapers and magazines, and campaigning essays in the quarterlies and monthlies, offered a pathway to prominence to an even wider group, including women such as Frances Power Cobbe. Otherwise journalistic celebrity was associated especially with the war correspondents, most notably W. H. Russell of *The Times* and Archibald Forbes, both of whom enjoyed a successful secondary career on the lecture platform.

The standing of the leading proponents of its various branches tells us a great deal about the hierarchies of Victorian literary culture. Fiction, and above all the novel, remained the Victorians' crowning glory. Selections inevitably varied but few would have disputed that the most admired novelists included Dickens, George Eliot, and Hardy, and to them most would have added the Brontë sisters, Gaskell, Thackeray, Trollope, and perhaps R. L. Stevenson. And this leaves out not only those just beginning to make a name in the 1890s, including John Galsworthy, Arnold Bennett, and H. G. Wells, but also a whole range of others, those like Charles Kingsley, Edward Bulwer-Lytton, and Charles Reade who were occasionally placed amongst the Victorian greats, a slew of more popular writers, many of whom have obtained a place in the modern canon of Victorian literature, including Wilkie Collins, Arthur Conan Doyle, Mrs Humphry Ward, and also C. M. Yonge, Mrs Oliphant (who contributed almost 100 novels on her own), and Ouida, and an army of writers who fed the fiction-consuming demands of the circulating libraries and the periodical press and enjoyed considerable contemporary fame before passing almost immediately into obscurity.

Poets had a more subordinate status. Tennyson was unchallenged, although Robert Browning was often close behind, and in particular places and periods Matthew Arnold, William Morris, A. C. Swinburne, and Rudyard Kipling also had their champions. Poetry was also an area where the female voice was less likely to be marginalized, although the conventional sentimentality of contemporary favourites, like the Queen's own, Adelaide Proctor, has generally been superseded in the modern canon by the more critical voices and richer identity politics of Christina Rossetti, Amy Levy, Mathilde Blind, and 'Michael Field' (the nom de plume of the partnership of Katherine Bradley and her niece Edith Cooper), or the experimentation of Gerard Manley Hopkins, most of whose poems remained unpublished until the following century.

In comparison, drama was a very poor cousin, and music perhaps an embarrassing minor family branch. Many literary figures dabbled in acting, most famously Dickens. But for most of the period, as illustrated by the career of Dion Boucicault, play-writing was largely hack-work, adapting domestic novels or foreign plays, with a focus especially in the mid-Victorian decades on spectacle rather than script. Only towards the end of the period did the more 'serious' plays of Arthur Wing Pinero and Henry Arthur Jones attract praise, although even the best of their work (such as Pinero's *The Second Mrs Tanqueray* (1893)) has survived primarily as period pieces. With the exception of J. M. Barrie's *Peter Pan*, only the acerbic social comedies of Wilde and the tract-plays of George Bernard Shaw have truly endured, and in both cases the reputations of the writers rest on much more than their dramatic work. In the same way, although Victorian musical cultures were both varied and vibrant, even the most effusive of contemporary assessments could find little to celebrate by way of British achievement. The most popular contemporary composers and conductors were continental, and although by the very end of the reign Edward Elgar and Ralph Vaughan Williams were beginning to change this, before 1900 the comic operas of Gilbert and Sullivan had to do service for a successful indigenous musical culture.

In some respects Victorian art and architecture were also backwaters, standing largely aloof from the main European currents. The Victorian art world was a chaos of coteries, schools, and styles from the moral-purpose art of Augustus Egg, and the sentimental genre paintings of Richard Redgrave, through the social realism of Hubert Herkomer to the sometimes brutal modernist impressionism of the Anglo-German Walter Sickert. By far the most celebrated grouping was the Pre-Raphaelite Brotherhood, and especially William Holman Hunt, whose highly finished moralism appealed to a new constituency of middle-class buyers, and John Edward Millais, whose later paintings gained even wider presence as adverts (perhaps most famously his *Bubbles*, used for a Pears soap advertisement (Figure 5)). The Brotherhood's main advocate, Ruskin, also championed the remarkable vision of J. M. W. Turner, and the Gothic revival in architecture, which was the nearest the Victorians came to a distinctive architectural style, most magnificently represented in A. W. Pugin's Houses of Parliament and Alfred Waterhouse's Natural History Museum: an aesthetic which also infused the arts and crafts furnishings and objects of William Morris and William de Morgan, and even the art nouveau of Charles Rennie Mackintosh.

The Victorians were adept at finding pleasure not only in commercial entertainment, but also in the serious business of politics and religion. The press and platform brought leading figures of both into a direct relationship with Victorian audiences no other fields could rival. The impact of the great Victorian orators and preachers is especially elusive. For a few, including John Henry Newman or the Scottish evangelical Thomas Chalmers, it survives in the significance of their ideas. But for most, including Charles Haddon Spurgeon, the most popular Victorian preacher of all, their purely performative appeal remains ephemeral and ungraspable, their ability to hold audiences for hours at a time another of the aspects of the Victorian condition entirely alien to modern sensibilities. Much the same could be said of the famous Victorian actors and theatrical impresarios, like William Macready, Charles Kean, and Sir Henry Irving, whose

5. Pears Soap advert based on J. E. Millais, *Bubbles* (*c*.1888–9).

mannered performances sound, in contemporary description at least, quite unlike the naturalism that later audiences came to expect.

In comparison, the emerging spectator sports of the later reign did not really produce national sporting stars. Such celebrities as there were continued to come, like the cricketer W. G. Grace and the jockey Fred Archer, from the traditional gentlemanly sports. Although someone like the prize fighter Tom Sayers, who retired with a public subscription of £3,000, anticipated the broad-appeal celebrity of 20th-century mass culture, it was not sport but the expanding commercial music hall of the 1880s which first created popular stars for the Victorian working classes, including the comedian/actor Dan Leno and the singer Marie Lloyd.

For people so aware of the technological advances that they were living through, the Victorians were surprisingly grudging in their scientific heroes, and even more reluctant in their recognition of industrialists and inventors. Photography, cinematography, and the bicycle all lacked the eureka moment which most easily brought individual fame, and many of the century's most striking subsequent innovations were developed overseas, including the typewriter, the phonogram, the telephone (although by the Scottish-born Alexander Graham Bell), and the internal combustion engine. As a result, the most prominent inventors in the late Victorian period were the armaments manufacturers William Armstrong and Joseph Whitworth, alongside Joseph Swan, inventor (in parallel with Thomas Edison) of the incandescent electric light bulb.

For the first half of the period geology and electricity were the two scientific fields of most significant advance, and the physicist Michael Faraday and the palaeontologist Richard Owen their leading representatives. In the middle decades evolutionary theory made Darwin the most notable of all Victorian scientists, even though he personally shunned the limelight, and the coterie of

Darwinians led by T. H. Huxley who formed the private X-Club attracted greater attention (as much for the theological implications of their scientific naturalism, and their penchant for controversy in the serious periodicals, as for their biology). By the final years of the century it was the sub-atomic physics represented by Joseph J. Thomson and Ernest Rutherford which was capturing the public imagination.

Conclusion

We gravitate to exemplary individuals for good reason: people make history and if we are to understand the Victorians we need to get to know some of them as flesh and blood, to appreciate their contributions, to recognize their perspectives, to understand their experiences, to see what makes them tick, and to gain insight into the diversity of their histories. But just as historical periods can't ever be fully encapsulated by representative individuals we must not fall into the trap of thinking that the Victorians can be 'characterized' through a handful of personalities. It was the experience of the often named but regularly counted masses which ultimately hold the key to the Victorian condition. And nowhere was this more so than in the global presence of the Victorians.

Chapter 7
The Victorian world

Where was Victorian?

It's an enquiry that spreads across three concentric questions.
How far did even the nations of the British Isles share enough of a
culture in common to be collectively described as Victorian? How
'Victorian' was the empire, both in its white 'British' settlers and
their children, and the variously 'Anglicized' indigenous
inhabitants. And to what degree was Victorian Britain's global
presence so pronounced as to involve the implanting of Victorian
characteristics in other parts of the world? And all this of course
also opens up the reverse question: how far was what we see as
Victorian in reality the outcome of two-way processes of
engagement and exchange with the wider world?

The drive to give full attention to their international and global
contexts has probably been the most powerful impetus in the
study of the Victorians in recent years. The idea of British
'exceptionalism', so powerful for the Victorians themselves, has
been largely discounted. We now recognize that Britain in the 19th
century shared many of its underlying structural conditions with
the rest of the western world, and can only be fully understood
when considered as part of a set of relationships and influences
which transcended its borders and its obvious spheres of
influence.

Even so, our starting point should be that 'Victorian' is not a natural label beyond Britain; not just because of its association with the particularities of the British monarchy, but because Britain *was* different. The Channel, as reflected in John Brett's paintings of the 1880s and 1890s, like *Britannia's Realm* (1880) (Figure 6), operated for many Victorians as a cultural and military moat. British 'exceptionalism' may have always been as much a matter of the performance of national stereotypes as of underlying realities, but it was none the less deeply engrained for that. *Punch* supplied the Victorians with a constant diet of cartoons (Figure 7) in which 'John Bull' as a personification of the national character, down to earth, commonsensical, hard-working, assertive, and suspicious of foreigners, faced off against the lumbering and aggressive Russian Bear or shifty 'Uncle Sam'. Works such as Emerson's *English Traits* (1856) and the series of tongue-in-cheek national studies produced by 'Max O'Rell' (Paul Blouet) in the 1880s, including *John Bull and his Island* (1883), reinforced contemporaries' belief in everyday differences of attitude and behaviour. And undoubtedly these did reflect fundamental underlying contrasts: more confined government, more vital religious institutions, less divorce and illegitimacy, much greater social and therefore political stability, even the different emphases

6. John Brett, *Britannia's Realm* (1880).

"HOLD ON, JOHN!"

7. 'Hold on John', *Punch* (2 April 1898).

of intellectual life. Almost wherever you look in Victorian Britain national peculiarities stare back.

This is not to endorse the stereotype of 'little Englandism', the cliché that the Victorians pitied continentals for the misfortune of not being British, that they measured the deficiencies of other cultures in the degrees to which they diverged from British modes. Relations were much richer than this. At the risk of replacing one set of prejudices with an only slightly more refined set, Victorian Britain demonstrated an intellectual obligation and at times deference to Germany, an emotional investment in Italy, and not infrequently a fear of France, military and moral, which the allure of Paris and the Riviera only partially dispelled. The Continent offered many less orthodox Victorians of the middle and upper classes opportunities and freedoms unavailable in Britain. They journeyed to study in Germany, climb in Switzerland, immerse themselves in Classical civilization in Italy, or holiday on the Riviera, and brought powerful intellectual influences back. Often, as in the case of the Brownings and Vernon Lee in Florence, Edward Lear at San Remo, or J. A. Symonds in Davos, long-term residence on the Continent brought a sense of belonging that Britain could not supply. Even so, 'abroad' was still frequently conceived of as irredeemably alien and exotic, a source of low morals and political extremism, an example of indolence and stagnation.

Cultural superciliousness was never allowed to become diplomatic isolationism. Victorian policy-makers were inclined to bluster and bully, but they were rarely able to impose or ignore. The Napoleonic wars had demonstrated that Britain 'ruled the waves'; but its creaking naval supremacy allowed invasion to rival revolution as a source of national anxiety. Despite the best efforts of the anti-war radicalism of the Manchester School, powerful currents of chauvinism encouraged Victorian policy-makers to meet insecurity with aggression. Even after withdrawing from the formal concert of powers which had attempted to manage post-Napoleonic Europe, Britain remained committed to maintaining the balance of power, and its overarching stance was less the 'splendid isolation' often suggested, and more interference without entanglements. Salisbury's famous observation that British policy was 'to float lazily downstream, occasionally putting out a diplomatic boat hook to avoid collisions', although it deliberately downplayed the frequency and violence of the boat hooks, contained a great deal of truth. Strategic concern for the supply lines to India which flowed through the Middle East meant a particular desire to keep Russia out of the Eastern Mediterranean through support for the increasingly dysfunctional Ottoman Empire, and this drew Britain into interventions in an ever-widening regional sphere, especially after the opening of the Suez Canal in 1869.

Internal empire

English superiority also operated within the British Isles, in ways that raise questions about how far all of Britain was 'Victorian'. It is important to remember that Victorian Britain was a loosely integrated polity comprising four nations, in which an overarching national identity had only recently been forged. After all, it was only in 1800 that the Act of Union had formally absorbed Ireland into the British polity and abolished the Dublin parliament. The 'Celtic nations' were well represented in British politics and public life, and internal migration and intermarriage meant that relations were always as much a matter of fusion as friction. At the start of the reign the population of England was barely 50 per cent of the total population of Britain, and in the later 19th century 30 per cent of the population of Liverpool were of Irish extraction. Victoria played her part, with her regular visits to Balmoral and the publication of her *Highland Diaries*, although she was much less inclined to visit Ireland or Wales. And W. E. Gladstone symbolizes the consequences: entirely Scottish by descent, a Liverpool merchant, he married into a Welsh family, inherited an estate in North Wales, and represented four different English and one Scottish constituency during his long parliamentary career.

Scotland especially benefited from this integration, retaining, unlike Wales, a separate legal system, a distinctive religious landscape, and its own legislation; in contrast Wales and Ireland were still, in the words of the historian John Seeley, the 'inner empire'. Wales was a largely invisible addendum to England for almost all the period, its distinctive cultural traditions ignored, an irrelevance in politics, mired in the view of Matthew Arnold in archaic resistance to the 'despotism of fact'. Ireland shared the potential benefits of absorption into the British polity only fitfully and partially. And each of the nations was itself variegated with its own minorities: Highland Scots, Ulster Protestants, and Welsh-speakers from North and Central Wales.

The idea of 'Victorian Ireland' raises particular challenges. While the Protestant families of the 'Ascendancy' mixed easily with English society, Irish Catholic elites were never fully reconciled to British rule, and landless agricultural workers resented the semi-feudal structures through which they were exploited by absentee landlords and abused by their agents. While the Sligo landlord Henry Temple could serve in government, as Lord Palmerston, almost continuously from 1809 to 1865, and although a succession of Irish novelists and playwrights were able to establish themselves at the heart of the London literary scene, many of the English had little knowledge of Ireland and for most of the Irish British rule was experienced as a matter of distance and neglect. Disraeli never visited; even Gladstone, for whom Ireland became the fulcrum of his politics, went there only once. It was always more of a dependency than a consolidated part of the kingdom, separated by religion and society, economically subordinate and politically subject in ways neither Scotland nor Wales were.

In the rest of Britain the 'ordinary Irish' were represented by the powerful racial stereotype of 'Paddy': uncouth, unclean, uncivilized, for the contemporary English historian J. A. Froude 'more like squalid apes than human beings'. When it suited the government in London, and it often did, Ireland was treated as a distinct political entity. As social and political unrest spread Ireland was policed like a colony, with martial law. Even attempts to respond to Irish demands by granting greater self-government were conceived as the sort of 'responsible government' which had been conceded to the settler colonies.

Global Britain

Of course such frames of reference serve to remind us of the extent to which Victorian Britain was a global polity. Not least as a result of the profits it had extracted from the Atlantic slave trade, and continued to enjoy from the processing of slave-grown cotton,

Victorian Britain was the pre-eminent imperial superpower of the 19th century. In economic terms Britain's dominance, even though there was inevitably some relative decline, remained unassailable; but in military terms British hegemony was always fragile and threatened, and the expansion of the empire was always as much a function of weakness as of strength.

However cautious we need to be in talking about an 'industrial revolution', there is no doubt that by the early years of Victoria's reign Britain had secured an extraordinary lead over the rest of the world in the new heavy industries. In the 1840s Britain was producing 65 per cent of the entire global output of coal, 70 per cent of the world's steel, and even 45 per cent of the more widely produced iron, and in 1881 was still the source of almost half the world's exported manufactures. Thereafter Britain's undisputed dominance was eroded, but not decisively overthrown. British cotton textiles from Lancashire and woollen textiles from Yorkshire dominated markets throughout Asia and South America. There were over 1,500 British mercantile houses operating across the world by the later 1840s, and by the following decade 60 per cent of global ocean shipping tonnage was registered in Britain, a figure that did not fall below 50 per cent until after 1901. A dynamic firm like the Jardine Matheson company was able to build an extensive portfolio of trading and manufacturing interests across Asia.

Ultimately, though, the Victorians' global presence inhered more in investment than in trade or manufacturing. By the 1850s Britain was investing £30 million p.a. overseas, and in the three decades up to 1900 the accumulated value of these investments doubled to nearly £2,000 million. No other country came close to these sorts of figures. Only a small portion went to the British empire (and most of that to India); the rest flowed to the United States, to Central and South America, and to Asia. The institutions and instruments required to lubricate all this activity, and the immense profits available, made London the financial capital of the world. This intricately interconnected network of merchant banks, insurance houses, shipping lines, and mercantile firms formed the basis of the great wealth and influence of what has come to be described as 'gentlemanly capitalism'.

Victorian Britain's expansionism was not just a matter of profit but also of people and principles. Although Britain had lost most of its North American empire in the 18th century it entered the Victorian period with extensive colonial territories in what were eventually to become Canada, Australia, the West Indies, and India, as well as a network of naval bases and trading posts, quickly extended by the foundation of the colony of New Zealand in 1840, and the acquisition of Hong Kong in 1842. But these acquisitions were not evidence of any coherent imperial design. In the early years of the reign, energized by the abolition of slavery, the most active impetus for British global action probably came from the powerful missionary organizations which inspired Victorians like David Livingstone with a vision of bringing Christianity and civilization to those parts of the world still sunk in 'savagery' and 'barbarism'.

Over the course of the century as many as 10 million people left Britain for a new life overseas. To give a sense of the scale, perhaps 40 per cent of those born in Britain in 1871 would emigrate during their lives. Emigration was a routine part of the Victorian experience, although especially for the Irish, driven from their homes in large numbers by the Potato Famine of 1845–9. Emigration was institutionalized by trades unions and supported by agents, promoters, and philanthropists. Few families were unaffected; four of Dickens's seven sons emigrated; Matthew Arnold had brothers in India and Australia.

As with finance these were not primarily flows to the empire. As many as two-thirds of the emigrants went to the United States, and the British population of Buenos Aires at the end of the century was still larger than the entire white settler populations of Kenya and Northern and Southern Rhodesia combined. Many also had no intention of staying permanently; they were missionaries, soldiers, administrators, merchants, gold prospectors, refugees, and adventurers, and probably more than a third of those who moved to live abroad returned at some point.

Expansion came reluctantly rather than enthusiastically. At least initially, suspicion of the consequences of formal annexations of territory and a desire to avoid expense dominated. Before the 1880s empire was a small and sleepy backwater of government. Much of Britain's global hegemony was 'informal empire'. Force was used where needed to obtain commercial access but formal control was avoided wherever possible. In China 'treaty ports' upheld the rights of European traders. In South America, and especially in Argentina, anglophone elites, educated at English public schools, sharing British consumer tastes, committed themselves and their countries to British economic standards, and shared investment control of railways, banks, mines, and utilities.

Elsewhere, indigenous societies were often either so entirely destabilized as to create a vacuum of order into which British actors on the periphery were inexorably drawn, or sufficiently powerful to reach a point at which they sought to resist further encroachments on their political or economic autonomies by force of arms. In both cases the interests of 'stability' often led to piecemeal expansion. Insufficiently restrained ambition on the frontier was met with resigned acceptance at home.

The violence of these processes makes a mockery of Seeley's suggestion that for much of the period empire was acquired in a fit of 'absence of mind'. Britain was involved almost continuously in warfare, in a way that cannot be captured even by a full list of imperial conflicts, from the Opium wars with China in the

1840s and 1850s, wars on the north-west frontier of India in the 1840s and 1880s, to the Southern Africa wars from the late 1870s. There were innumerable small anti-insurrectionary wars, along the lines of the Benin expedition of 1897 which sacked Benin city and led to the incorporation of the kingdom into colonial Nigeria. The fact that 'The civiliser's spade grinds horribly | On dead men's bones', as Elizabeth Barrett Browning put it in *Aurora Leigh* (1856), although often occluded, could never be entirely hidden.

Maps of the empire on which the sun never set, coloured in uniform red, gave the Victorian empire an entirely spurious appearance of unity. In reality it was a chaos of different jurisdictions with little in the way of central coordination, without logic, united by little more than Britain's underlying willingness to assert its authority with violence and bloodshed. It was not until later in the reign that explicit manifestos, like Seeley's *The Expansion of England* (1883) and Froude's *Oceana or England and her Colonies* (1886), offered a positive view of the colonies as part of British national destiny and a space where Anglo-Saxon culture could renew itself. Even then, campaigns for greater imperial consolidation, like the Imperial Federation League (1884), gained little public traction.

What there was instead was an imperial mindset, an assumption of British superiority, an expectation of global conquest. The settler colonies, largely treated as if they had had no previous populations, achieved significant autonomy early in the reign. India, South-East Asia, and later parts of Africa were governed indirectly through indigenous rulers, involving elaborate rituals of intrigue and manoeuvre. Many smaller territories with the status of crown colonies were ruled autocratically by British representatives on the assumption that they lacked one or more of the attributes required even for the possibility of independence at some distant future date.

Victorians abroad

For the Salvation Army founder General William Booth, the white settler colonies were 'simply pieces of Britain distributed about the world', but although colonial society often appears to be an exotic facsimile of England, we must not think of this migration as spreading Victorian civilization in any sort of uncomplicated way. Emigrants were often motivated by a desire to escape from British conditions, and there was always the danger of 'going native'. (Frederick Maning, one early settler in New Zealand, described himself as 'a loyal subject to Queen Victoria' but 'also a member of a Maori tribe'.)

This said, the encounter with indigenous cultures often pushed settlers back towards particularly aggressive versions of Englishness. Etiquette and social conventions were maintained even if entirely unsuited to the climate. Religious and sectarian tensions were exported. Mechanics' institutes, libraries, and clubs were created in the image of 'home'. British news filled colonial newspapers. The Indian hill station of Simla, with its clubs, balls, fetes, and fun-fairs, was described by the painter Val Prinseps as just like Margate. Much the same can be said of places where the British population was confined to a smaller elite of merchants, soldiers, and administrators, where the sense of cultural isolation often produced even greater hyper-policing of orthodoxies.

This was not a version of Victorian culture accessible to the colonized, no matter what imperial ideologies might say. And in any case, confidence in Britain's 'civilizing mission' ebbed steadily away as the century progressed. Aspiration for improvement slipped easily into a preoccupation with backwardness, lip-service to the desire to protect and preserve being undermined by the exploitation of mineral resources or the imposition of plantation economies. Instead of education and assimilation, the boundaries between colonizer and colonized were reinforced by carefully ritualized, even if rarely absolute, segregation. The greater the westernized element of colonized populations, the more entrenched the separatism. Indian railway stations had separate dining rooms for Hindus, Muslims, and Europeans. However carefully Indians might adopt the British language and British mores, they were always marked as inferior, and there was little mixing outside the confines of purely official business.

Not that we should imagine that it was ever an aspiration of the colonized simply to become 'Victorians'. Their responses, even when they fell short of the sustained rejection of the Māoris, for example, were always a combination of resistance and accommodation. Empire generated a cadre of local collaborators, translators, advisers, and low-level administrators who valued the accoutrements of Victorian culture, or at least the opportunities the imperial presence provided. Indian princes sent their children to local simulacra of the English public school, and sometimes on to Eton or Oxford. Even in the settler colonies where there was less call for collaborating elites, indigenous populations developed their own (limited) Victorianism, in which the style of British subjects might be adopted as protection against appropriation and exploitation. The defeated Zulu Cetshwayo kaMpande dressed in British clothes and 'performed' such a role during his visit to England in 1882. But although they may have become partially 'Anglicized', these colonized elites were never facsimile Victorians. They retained their own cultures and languages alongside their 'Englishness'. Theirs was less an imitative flattery and more an instrumental mimicry, often aiming quite consciously at relative advantage in the short term and resistance in the longer.

If this was the case within the empire, what are we to make of the suggestion, never widespread, but common enough, that we can use 'Victorian' as a designation for nations and societies beyond the empire, that we can talk about 'Victorian Russia' or 'Victorian Americans'? These labels do not seek to suggest that other nations shared Britain's Victorian periodization, but by drawing on the familiar playbook of Victorianism, they try to identify common components of 19th-century cultures. And there is no doubt that elements of Victorian culture circulated widely. Smiles's *Self-Help* was a global phenomenon, widely translated, and a particular favourite in sometimes unlikely places, including Japan. But this is not the same as suggesting that 'Victorian' might be a broadly applicable designation.

The difficulties are illustrated by Tolstoy's *Anna Karenina* (1878). Superficially, with its references to English literature, English carriages, billiards, and lawn tennis, the novel describes the penetration of English culture into Russian life; but it also reflects the narrowness and artificiality of these always alien intrusions. Even in the strongest candidate, America, which shared Britain's biblical evangelicalism, common law, Anglo-Saxonism, and the celebration of individual and collective improvement, the differences were profound. Americans certainly read and reacted to the Victorians: it was cheaper for publishers to pirate Dickens and Trollope than to pay royalties to Hawthorne or Poe, and British celebrities were regularly lionized on the American lecture circuit. But they rarely simply imitated them, as the comparison between the newspaper presses or the political systems of the two countries and the discomfort, not infrequently sliding into distaste, of many English visitors makes clear.

Empire at home

It may well have been, as some historians have argued, that empire impinged surprisingly little on the direct consciousness and preoccupations of Victorian public culture. Even India, despite the pageantry of Victoria's installation as empress in 1876, remained largely a problem for administrators rather than for politicians. Even so, empire soaked deep into the fabric of everyday life. The appetite for acquisition may have been fickle, but once acquired imperial possessions became a source of pride, an affirmation of Britain's favoured status. At moments of crisis, such as the 'Indian Mutiny' or the Boer War, empire engrossed public attention. At other times engagement was less overt but nonetheless pervasive. Imperial vocabularies enriched the language. Empire fed Victorian exhibitionary culture and the constant parade of colonial 'natives' and 'tribal life' which were part of stage and periodicals. Global exchanges lurked at the margins of Victorian literature, and indeed the returned emigrant, imperial trophy, or colonial wealth were frequently at the very heart of its plots. As the period progressed imperial adventure became a stock genre of boys' magazines. Artists celebrated Britain's maritime strength and overseas expansion. Advertisers emblazoned empire on soap wrappings, biscuit tins, chocolate bars, and whisky bottles.

Empire was always much more than its overt presences or manifestations. It played a constitutive role in Victorian culture, albeit one that was often encrypted, taking place off stage, just as the profits of slavery were consolidated into bricks and mortar, financial instruments and philanthropic endowments, in the Tate Gallery, Rhodes Scholarships, and the Joseph Rowntree Foundation. Global power sustained a general belief in the superiority of British culture and institutions, and infused strains of hierarchy, narrow-mindedness, and an increasingly militarist masculinity. Empire functioned as a site for exploration of contemporary anxieties, such as the 'new woman', re-imagined by Rider Haggard's *She* as an all-powerful sorceress. Contemporary idiom was charged with imperial resonances. References to 'darkest England', 'home missions', or 'street arabs' all indicate the ways in which domestic social problems were framed by imperial perspectives. By the end of the period there was a tendency to treat the white settler colonies as, in the words of Herbert Asquith, laboratories for 'political and social experiments'.

Balance sheets and moral judgements

Consideration of the Victorians' role in the wider 19th-century world raises in particularly acute ways judgements about costs and benefits, both impacts and legacies. What was the balance sheet of this globalization? The answer is not entirely straightforward, although espousal of the positive has come to be seen as morally unthinkable. It is easy to see why. For all the profession of altruistic intentions, empire was motivated by and systematically organized around the strategic and economic interests of the metropolis. The numbers who gained by western education or commerce were tiny, and principles of progress and equality were always subordinated to imperial expediency.

Forcible integration into the world economy played havoc with indigenous manufacturing, and left colonies at the mercy of global commodity prices. The 'drain of wealth' arguments Indian intellectuals were making by the end of the reign are impossible to ignore. It matters little that by the most sophisticated econometric measures the actual benefit Britain obtained from empire was marginal. Under empire disease ravaged Polynesians, famines killed over 10 million Indians, and in West Africa the imposition of commercial farming brought systemic economic vulnerability. It is hard to defend empire on the basis that it bore down on indigenous 'barbarism' with a barbarism of its own, or that it brought modernization by the forcible destruction of local economies. And even if this could be construed as a material gain, the underlying reality of subjugation and suppression would remain.

Yet a full accounting involves questioning of alternatives and a move beyond zero-sum calculations. Compromised as the argument is, the major benefit of the British empire may well have been preserving parts of the world from the even greater disaster of being part of the other European empires. Although subordinated to economic advantage, there was a powerful constitutionalist vision of British imperialism which both envisaged and actively worked for the advancement of indigenous inhabitants, and produced a genuine desire for improvement from administrators like Lord Curzon and local officials like Leonard Woolf, and the dissemination of culture, language, and technology, the democratic ideal of disinterested public service and representative governance. To dismiss all as merely destructive is to ignore the conditioned agency of at least some of the colonized, and the complicated heritages of nationalism and nationhood which endured. The question of whether these were entirely insignificant in the context of the horrors of empire ultimately depends on the almost impossible judgement of whether without empire similar horrors would have been avoided.

Conclusion

Such questions return us to where we started. The Victorian empire was no different from the rest of Victorian Britain, incomprehensible if approached in search of simple categorization. Like the Victorians who maintained and extended it, it was a mass of contradictions, a force for ill and for good, a machine of violence and of order. It has long been history and yet its legacies have stubbornly endured, unconfined to the glass case of past experience. Perhaps, because ambivalence and embarrassment have discouraged attempts to fully explore, never mind to come to terms with, its complexities, it is the one aspect of the Victorians about which we do not know too much. But we should be wary of allowing colonialism to become our version of 'Victorianism', freighted purely with negative connotation. Ultimately in the case of empire, as the Victorians have helped demonstrate more generally, attempting to construct historical understanding out of moral categories leads at best to distortion and often to misunderstanding. The importance of the Victorians will continue to be in large part a matter of how we feel, but our feelings are a poor guide to Victorian history or to the Victorians' legacies.

References

Chapter 1: The challenge of generalization

'The history...it': Lytton Strachey, *Eminent Victorians* (2003), 5.
'agreed...detail': John Darwin, *Unfinished Empire: The Global Expansion of Britain* (2012), 278.

Chapter 2: Living with the Victorians

'We...Victorian': David Paul, 'The Public Taste', *The Twentieth Century* 151 (1952), 253.
'a tireless...century': John Major, *The Autobiography* (1999), 1.
'very...community', and 'a bit...Victorian': Asa Briggs, quoted in Daniel Snowman, 'Asa Briggs', *History Today* 49 (October 1999), 3.
'Victorian-ness...we live': Matthew Sweet, *Inventing the Victorians* (2001), xxii.
'Crying went out and the cold bath came in | with drains, bananas, bicycles and tin': W. H. Auden, 'Letter to Lord Byron' (1936).
'yearning...buoyancy': Basil Willey, *Nineteenth Century Studies* (1949), 51–2.
'When...Roebuck': Roy Hattersley, 'Nothing new under the Millennium Dome: Endpiece', *Guardian*, 5 January 1998, 14.
'courage and refreshment': Guy Kendall, *Charles Kingsley and His Ideas* (1947), 9.
'to do...stand for': Philip Davis, *Why Does Victorian Literature Still Matter?* (2008), 156.
'fictionalised...facts': Malcolm Bradbury, *Cuts* (1987), 13.
'There...life': John Ruskin, *Unto this Last* (1862), 219.

'If we…confused': Morse Peckham, 'Can "Victorian" Have a Useful Meaning?', *Victorian Studies* 10 (March 1967), 277.

Chapter 3: The Victorian as period

'a giant paperweight…men's minds': H. G. Wells, quoted in Norman and Jeanne Mackenzie, eds, *The Diary of Beatrice Webb. Volume II 1892–1905: 'All the Good Things of Life'* (1983), 3.

'except in…ideologically unacceptable': John Lucas, 'Republican versus Victorian: Radical Writing in the Later Years of the Nineteenth Century', in J. Johns and A. Jenkins, eds, *Rethinking Victorian Culture* (2000), 29.

'lived in…languages': Sir James Mackintosh quoted in V. M. Lester, *Victorian Insolvency: Bankruptcy, Imprisonment for Debt, and Company Winding-up in Nineteenth Century Britain* (1995), 40.

'had a…victory': A. V. Dicey, quoted in N. Rance, *Wilkie Collins and Other Sensation Novelists* (1991), 23.

'anxious and high-minded 1870s': Kathryn Hughes, *Victorians Undone* (2017), 176.

'The centre…new': Joseph Chamberlain quoted in R. Shannon, *The Crisis of Imperialism* (1974), 185.

'spectatorial lust': J. A. Hobson, quoted in Annie Coombes, *Reinventing Africa: Museums, Material Culture and Popular Imagination* (1994), 63.

'living in…and 1900': James Bryce quoted in C. Harvie, *The Lights of Liberalism: University Liberals and the Challenge of Democracy, 1860–1886* (1976), 218.

'there…the year': '1901', *The Times*, 31 December 1901, 7.

'a murmuring groan…tears' and 'supremely…period': John Galsworthy, *The Forsyte Saga* (1922), 512, 518.

'lost much…of life': quoted in J. Schneer, *London in 1900: The Imperial Metropolis* (1999), 167.

Chapter 4: Victorianism

'Victorianism…a myth': G. M. Young, *Victorian England: Portrait of an Age* (2nd edn., 1953), p. vii.

'toss…yield': Havelock Ellis, quoted in C. Decker, *The Victorian Conscience* (1952), 179.

'fear of…odd': William Johnston, quoted in W. Houghton, *Victorian Frame of Mind* (1957), 398.

'the detailed...society': Robert Roberts, *The Classic Slum* (1971), 26.

'It is...into men': William Landels, *How Men Are Made* (1859), 43.

'rule of Ought': H. C. G. Matthew, ed., *The Gladstone Diaries*, VIII (1982), 163.

'peremptory and absolute': Eliot, quoted in G. Haight, *George Eliot: A Biography* (1968), 464.

'We are on the side of progress': T. B. Macaulay, 'Sir James Mackintosh: History of the Revolution', in Hannah Trevelyan, ed., *The Works of Lord Macaulay*, VI (1866), 90.

'lust for profusion': Charles Eastlake, quoted in Thad Logan, *The Victorian Parlour: A Cultural Study* (2001), 134.

William Morris, 'hatred...confusion', and E. P. Thompson, 'one of...written': E. P. Thompson, *William Morris: Romantic to Revolutionary* (1955), 153–4.

Chapter 5: Victorian configurations

'age of discussion': Walter Bagehot, *Physics and Politics* (1873), 156.

'Nothing...what not': *Bradford Observer*, 5 October 1868, cited in J. Tosh, *A Man's Place: Masculinity and the Middle-Class Home in Victorian England* (2007), 132.

'commercial atmosphere' and 'redolent...shop': Henry Mansel, 'Sensation Novels', *Quarterly Review* 113 (April 1863), 357.

'thoughts that shake mankind': Tennyson, 'Locksley Hall' (1835), first published in *Poems* (1842).

'completely...character': Gideon Mantell, quoted in Dennis R. Dean, *Gideon Mantell and the Discovery of Dinosaurs* (1999), 261.

'between...belief': Lord Acton, quoted in Ruth Solie, *Music in Other Worlds: Victorian Conversations* (2004), 159.

'must...no': A. Trollope, *An Autobiography* (1883), II, 35.

'the...character': Martin Wiener, *Reconstructing the Criminal: Culture, Law and Policy in England, 1830–1914* (1994), 11.

'mingled mass...pleasures': *The Times*, 20 June 1876, quoted in Peter Bailey, *Leisure and Class in Victorian England: Rational Recreation and the Contest for Control, 1830–1885* (1978), 56.

'absurdly...in machinery': Matthew Arnold, *Culture and Anarchy* (1869), 11.

'culture of looking': Isobel Armstrong, 'Transparency: Towards a Poetics of Glass in the Nineteenth Century', in Francis Spufford and Jenny Uglow, eds, *Cultural Babbage: Technology, Time and Invention* (1996), 125.

'frenzy of the visible': Jean Louis Comolli, 'Machines of the Visible', in Teresa de Laurentis and Stephen Heath, eds, *The Cinematic Apparatus* (1980), 122–3.

'stale...straw': quoted in Lee Jackson, *Dirty Old London* (2014), 1.

'stifling...hot oil': Charles Dickens, *Hard Times* (1858), 304.

Chapter 6: Eminent and less eminent Victorians

'the essence of innumerable biographies': Thomas Carlyle, 'On History', in Chris van den Bossche, ed., *Historical Essays: The Norman and Charlotte Strouse Edition of the Writings of Thomas Carlyle* (2002), 5.

Chapter 7: The Victorian world

'to float...collisions': Lord Salisbury, quoted in T. G. Otte, '"Floating Downstream?": Lord Salisbury and British Foreign Policy, 1878–1902', in T. G. Otte, *The Makers of British Foreign Policy* (2001), 98.

the 'despotism of fact': Matthew Arnold, quoted by Kenneth O. Morgan, *Modern Wales: Politics, Places and People* (1995), 4.

Froude, 'more like squalid apes than human beings': quoted in Nick Pelling, *Anglo-Irish Relations, 1798–1922* (2003), 33.

'The civiliser's...bones': Elizabeth Barrett Browning, *Aurora Leigh* (1856), Book 2, 53.

'simply...world': General William Booth, quoted in G. R. Searle, *A New England: Peace and War 1886–1918* (2004), 25.

Maning, 'a loyal...Victoria' and 'also...tribe': quoted in Patrick Brantlinger, *Victorian Literature and Postcolonial Studies* (2009), 86.

Herbert Asquith, 'political...experiments': quoted in A. Thompson, *The Empire Strikes Back? The Impact of Imperialism on Britain from the Mid-Nineteenth Century* (2005), 144.

Further reading

Chapter 2: Living with the Victorians

Dinah Birch, *Our Victorian Education* (2008)

Philip Davis, *Why Does Victorian Literature Still Matter?* (2008)

John Gardiner, *The Victorians: An Age in Retrospect* (2002)

Ann Heilmann and Mark Llewellyn, *Neo-Victorianism: The Victorians in the Twenty-First Century, 1999–2009* (2010)

Christine L. Krueger, ed., *Functions of Victorian Culture at the Present Time* (2002)

Lytton Strachey, *Eminent Victorians* (2003 edn; 1918)

Matthew Sweet, *Inventing the Victorians* (2001)

Miles Taylor and Michael Wolff, eds, *The Victorians Since 1901: Histories, Representations and Revisions* (2004)

Chapter 3: The Victorian as period

G. F. A. Best, *Mid-Victorian Britain, 1851–1875* (1993)

David Cannadine, *Victorious Century: Britain 1800–1906* (2018)

Jose Harris, *Private Lives, Public Spirit: Britain 1870–1914* (1993)

J. F. C. Harrison, *Early Victorian Britain, 1832–51* (2008)

J. F. C. Harrison, *Late Victorian Britain, 1875–1901* (1990)

Boyd Hilton, *A Mad, Bad and Dangerous People? England 1783–1846* (2006)

K. Theodore Hoppen, *The Mid-Victorian Generation, 1846–1886* (1998)

G. R. Searle, *A New England? Peace and War 1886–1918* (2004)

Robert Tombs, 'Victorian England' in his *The English and Their History* (2014)

Chapter 4: Victorianism

Richard Altick, *Victorian People and Ideas* (1973)

Asa Briggs, 'Victorianism', in Asa Briggs, *A Social History of England* (2nd edn, 1987)

Robin Gilmour, *The Victorian Period: The Intellectual and Cultural Context of English Literature, 1830–1890* (1993)

Walter Houghton, *The Victorian Frame of Mind* (1957)

Kathryn Hughes, *Victorians Undone: Tales of Flesh in the Age of Decorum* (2017)

Gordon Marsden, ed., *Victorian Values: Personalities and Perspectives in Nineteenth Century Society* (2nd edn, 1998)

David Newsome, *The Victorian World Picture* (1997)

M. J. D. Roberts, *Making English Morals: Voluntary Association and Moral Reform in England, 1787–1886* (2004)

Chapter 5: Victorian configurations

Simon Heffer, *High Minds: The Victorians and the Birth of Modern Britain* (2013)

Martin Hewitt, ed., *The Victorian World* (2012)

Theodore K. Hoppen, *The Mid-Victorian Generation, 1846–1886* (1998)

Richard Price, *British Society 1680–1880: Dynamism, Containment and Change* (1999)

Susie Steinbach, *Understanding the Victorians: Politics, Culture and Society in Nineteenth Century Britain* (2016)

M. Young, *Victorian England: Portrait of an Age* (1992; or. 1936)

Chapter 6: Eminent and less eminent Victorians

Juliet Atkinson, *Victorian Biography Reconsidered: A Study of Nineteenth Century 'Hidden Lives'* (2010)

Asa Briggs, *Victorian People* (1955)

David Gange, *The Victorians* (2016)

Kathryn Gleadle, *British Women in the Nineteenth Century* (2001)

Simon Goldhill, *A Very Queer Family Indeed: Sex, Religion and the Bensons in Victorian Britain* (2016)

Elizabeth Longford, *Eminent Victorian Women* (1981)

John Woolf and Keshia N. Abraham, *Black Victorians: Hidden in History* (2022)

Chapter 7: The Victorian world

James Belich, *Replenishing the Earth: The Settler Revolution and the Rise of Angloworld* (2011)

Patrick Brantlinger, *Rule of Darkness: British Literature and Imperialism, 1830–1914* (1988)

Caroline Elkins, *Legacy of Violence: A History of the British Empire* (2022)

Ashley Jackson, *The British Empire: A Very Short Introduction* (2013)

Andrew Porter, *The Nineteenth Century: Oxford History of the British Empire* (2001)

Andrew Thompson, *The Empire Strikes Back? The Impact of Imperialism on Britain from the Mid-Nineteenth Century* (2005)

Index

For the benefit of digital users, indexed terms that span two pages (e.g., 52–53) may, on occasion, appear on only one of those pages.

Index

ENGLISH LITERATURE
A Very Short Introduction
Jonathan Bate

Sweeping across two millennia and every literary genre, acclaimed scholar and biographer Jonathan Bate provides a dazzling introduction to English Literature. The focus is wide, shifting from the birth of the novel and the brilliance of English comedy to the deep Englishness of landscape poetry and the ethnic diversity of Britain's Nobel literature laureates. It goes on to provide a more in-depth analysis, with close readings from an extraordinary scene in King Lear to a war poem by Carol Ann Duffy, and a series of striking examples of how literary texts change as they are transmitted from writer to reader.

{No reviews}

www.oup.com/vsi

ROMANTICISM
A Very Short Introduction
Michael Ferber

What is Romanticism? In this *Very Short Introduction*
Michael Ferber answers this by considering who the romantics
were and looks at what they had in common – their ideas, beliefs,
commitments, and tastes. He looks at the birth and growth
of Romanticism throughout Europe and the Americas, and
examines various types of Romantic literature, music, painting,
religion, and philosophy. Focusing on topics, Ferber looks at the
rising prestige of the poet; Romanticism as a religious trend;
Romantic philosophy and science; Romantic responses to the
French Revolution; and the condition of women. Using examples
and quotations he presents a clear insight into this very diverse
movement.

www.oup.com/vsi

THE REFORMATION
A Very Short Introduction
Peter Marshall

The Reformation transformed Europe, and left an indelible mark on the modern world. It began as an argument about what Christians needed to do to be saved, but rapidly engulfed society in a series of fundamental changes. This *Very Short Introduction* provides a lively and up-to-date guide to the process. Peter Marshall argues that the Reformation was not a solely European phenomenon, but that varieties of faith exported from Europe transformed Christianity into a truly world religion. It explains doctrinal debates in a clear and non-technical way, but is equally concerned to demonstrate the effects the Reformation had on politics, society, art, and minorities.

www.oup.com/vsi

MODERNISM
A Very Short Introduction
Christopher Butler

Whether we recognise it or not, virtually every aspect of our life today has been influenced in part by the aesthetic legacy of Modernism. In this *Very Short Introduction* Christopher Butler examines how and why Modernism began, explaining what it is and showing how it has gradually informed all aspects of 20th and 21st century life. Butler considers several aspects of modernism including some modernist works; movements and notions of the avant garde; and the idea of 'progress' in art. Butler looks at modernist ideas of the self, subjectivity, irrationalism, people and machines, and political definitions of modernism as a whole.

www.oup.com/vsi

PROGRESSIVISM
A Very Short Introduction
Walter Nugent

This very timely *Very Short Introduction* offers an engaging
overview of progressivism in America--its origins, guiding
principles, major leaders and major accomplishments.
A many-sided reform movement that lasted from the late 1890s
until the early 1920s, progressivism emerged as a response
to the excesses of the Gilded Age, an era that plunged working
Americans into poverty while a new class of ostentatious
millionaires built huge mansions and flaunted their wealth.
Progressives fought for worker's compensation, child labour
laws, minimum wage and maximum hours legislation; they
enacted anti-trust laws, instituted the graduated income tax,
won women the right to vote, and laid the groundwork for
Roosevelt's New Deal.

www.oup.com/vsi

LATE ANTIQUITY
A Very Short Introduction
Gillian Clark

Late antiquity is the period (c.300–c.800) in which barbarian invasions ended Roman Empire in Western Europe by the fifth century and Arab invasions ended Roman rule over the eastern and southern Mediterranean coasts by the seventh century. Asking 'what, where, and when' Gillian Clark presents an introduction to the concept of late antiquity and the events of its time. Not only a period of cultural clashes, political restructurings, and geographical controversies, Clark also demonstrates the sheer richness and diversity of religious life as well as the significant changes to trade, economy, archaeology, and towns. Encapsulating significant developments through vignettes, she reflects upon the period by asking the question 'How much can we recognise in the world of late antiquity?'

www.oup.com/vsi

DRUIDS
A Very Short Introduction
Barry Cunliffe

The Druids first came into focus in Western Europe - Gaul, Britain, and Ireland - in the second century BC. They are a popular subject; they have been known and discussed for over 2,000 years and few figures flit so elusively through history. They are enigmatic and puzzling, partly because of the lack of knowledge about them has resulted in a wide spectrum of interpretations. Barry Cunliffe takes the reader through the evidence relating to the Druids, trying to decide what can be said and what can't be said about them. He examines why the nature of the druid caste changed quite dramatically over time, and how successive generations have interpreted the phenomenon in very different ways.

www.oup.com/vsi

FRENCH LITERATURE
A Very Short Introduction
John D. Lyons

The heritage of literature in the French language is rich,
varied, and extensive in time and space; appealing both to its
immediate public, readers of French, and also to aglobal
audience reached through translations and film adaptations.
French Literature: A Very Short Introduction introduces this lively
literary world by focusing on texts - epics, novels, plays, poems,
and screenplays - that concern protagonists whose adventures
and conflicts reveal shifts in literary and social practices. From
the hero of the medieval *Song of Roland* to the Caribbean
heroines of *Tituba, Black Witch of Salem* or the European
expatriate in Japan in *Fear and Trembling*, these problematic
protagonists allow us to understand what interests writers and
readers across the wide world of French.

SCIENCE FICTION
A Very Short Introduction
David Seed

Science Fiction has proved notoriously difficult to define. It has been explained as a combination of romance, science and prophecy; as a genre based on an imagined alternative to the reader's environment; and as a form of fantastic fiction and historical literature. It has also been argued that science fiction narratives are the most engaged, socially relevant, and responsive to the modern technological environment. This *Very Short Introduction* doesn't offer a history of science fiction, but instead ties examples of science fiction to different historical moments, in order to demonstrate how science fiction has evolved over time.